PERFECTLY
IMPERFECT

RAW REFLECTIONS ON BODY IMAGE,
MOTHERING, LOVE AND LONELINESS

(that you don't usually share)

AILSA ROBSON

First published in Australia in 2019 by
Boadicea Books
PO Box 284, Uraidla, SA. 5142
boadiceabooksaustralia@gmail.com

Copyright © Ailsa Robson 2019

Ailsa Robson asserts the moral right to be identified as the author of this work.

All rights reserved. No part of this book may be reproduced or transmitted by any person or entity (including Google, Amazon or similar organisations), in any form or by any means, electronic or mechanical, including photocopying, recording, scanning or by any information storage and retrieval system, without prior permission in writing from the publisher.

Cataloguing-in-Publication entry is available from the National Library of Australia

 A catalogue record for this book is available from the National Library of Australia

PERFECTLY IMPERFECT: Raw Reflections on Body Image, Mothering, Love and Loneliness (that you don't usually share) / Ailsa Robson

ISBN: 978-0-6483029-8-8 (paperback)
ISBN: 978-0-6483029-7-1 (epub)

Cover photography by Meaghan Coles
www.nowandthenphotography.com.au
Cover design by Tea Filipi www.betiobca.com
Layout and book typesetting by Sophie White
www.sophiewhite.com.au
Photos supplied by author unless otherwise stated.

Printed by Createspace

Disclaimer

This book is memoir. It reflects the author's recollections of experiences over time. Some names and characteristics have been changed, some events have been compressed, and some dialogue has been recreated. The author and publisher hereby exclude all liability to the extent permitted by law for any errors or omissions in this book and for any loss, damage or expense (whether direct or indirect) suffered by a third party relying on any information contained in this book.

WHAT READERS ARE SAYING

Loved it!!! This book will comfort so many women; especially pregnant/post pregnant mamas who are lost in the unglamorous, sleep deprived world of babies, whilst dealing with worries about their sassy but squishy post-pregnancy bods. Contrary to the 'perfect mums of Insta', and their contrived, unflawed worlds, this book is a breath of fresh air as it is raw and REAL. Motherhood can be a lonely, selfless, thankless task at times and this book warmly welcomes women into Ailsa's normal, genuine, crazy and flawed world. We all have our own shit going on, internally and externally; this story encompasses both and certainly gives some awesome takeaways about navigating an often intolerable, conceited world. It also aligns with my principles of believing in yourself, pushing outside of your comfort zone and never being afraid of following your dreams!

– **Jane,** *mother of 4 and kickass entrepreneur*

Ailsa is a bold, brave woman who epitomizes what it is to be woman – daughter, sister, mother, goddess and then some. Her wisdom and powerful vulnerability is born from experience. The telling of her journey from not feeling good enough to embracing her imperfections will take her readers by the hand and walk them through their own rebirth into self-loving acceptance. Sure to become the handbook of choice for so many woman as they heal their own body image and souls.

– **Leonie,** *psychotherapist, wellbeing educator and soul astrologer extraordinaire*

I loved this book! I found myself wanting to yell at Ailsa "for god's sake just let it go!" ('it' being the "perfect" body goal, and to notice how well it served her, not just its weight or what it looked like). Then I found myself squirming with the sense of how vulnerable she has made herself in examining so publicly her non-weight neutral-self. This book is going to speak to both clients and practitioners alike, especially those just coming to realise that maybe there is something other than our weight-centric way of practicing self-care.

– **Susan,** *Dietitian, HAES® activist and Mum*

This book spoke to me. So much of what Ailsa wrote, I could relate to in my life. Not just the parts about body image and weight-loss and the struggle to be perfect but also when she spoke about marriage and the struggle to keep romance alive when you have young kids and your focus is elsewhere. I loved when she spoke about the impact kids have on a marriage; the trashed house, the never-ending washing and chores, and business of life. The standout part for me was when she mentioned the line about "having someone to do nothing with". That was a 'yes' moment for me as this is what I have with my husband, he is my someone to do nothing with. I feel like I've made a new friend through reading this book.

– **Renee**, *wife and mother of 4, and well-travelled in her mind*

This book is for FIFO partners, and for the most part, women and mothers, who are interested in comparing like experiences, and seeking strategies or affirmations for the difficulties faced in family life. Whether you are a self-awareness journey-person, someone who enjoys diary/blog reading or simply curious folk, this book helps to keep it real, and lets others in on life where we can all be less than perfect mums, friends, partners or lovers. The vulnerability shown is a strength because everyone is facing their own version of pain/trauma/trouble… so quit judging!! For me, the key message in the book is to be compassionate to yourself and others.

– **Cate**, *a previous FIFO partner, mother of 4, RN, life-long learner and fabulously 50 already!!*

I felt very privileged to be invited to follow Ailsa's journey when she began writing her personal blog on which this book is based. It is raw, touching and inspiring. Her inner strength and ability to count her blessings sees her through some difficult situations of profound change, loss and grief – inspiring indeed. I admire Ailsa for sharing her deeply personal story with others. Her journey has resonated with me on many levels and I know other readers will feel the same.

– **Tania**, *artist, illustrator & lover of all fur-children*

To my darlings, Lily and Tess.

You are loved exactly as you are.

CONTENTS

What readers are saying	1
Foreword	9
Introduction	11
Timeline of influences	15
2009 – So Begins the Contemplation…	17
2010 – Body Changes / FIFO / Surprise / Sick	31
2011 – Mothering / Movement / Juggling / Lonesome	115
2012 – Running / Power / Change / Sass	147
2013 – Uni / Acceptance / Highs / Lows	181
2014 – Out of Steam…	201
Present Day Reflections	207
Jan 2018 – I am worthy of this space	213
Place and Privilege	215
About the author	217
Acknowledgments	219
References	220
Useful links	221
Glossary of terms	222
More from Ailsa Robson	223

FOREWORD

Ailsa writes: 'How far I have come...' What a courageous spirit Ailsa has to share such a personal part of her story, with the intention of helping others. Ailsa brings into the light a struggle so many people will be able to relate to, a struggle that is often life-long. Western Society, for various reasons, fosters issues around weight and body image, and fuels a range of "not good enough" stories.

I first met Ailsa whilst teaching on the Counselling and Psychotherapy training program that she so successfully completed. I remember Ailsa being a hungry student, attentive, soaking up all the information, and thoughtfully contributing to the classes. Her sassiness was evident then too, challenging others in the class about various opinions and issues, in her own respectful and considered way.

Ailsa also completed a placement in my practice, and after a week or two of observation, she started working with her own clients. Her confidence grew, and the clients genuinely appreciated being able to work with her. In fact, they loved Ailsa. She has "it" in terms of counselling – pure kindness towards others, a good mind, and the ability to pace the work in sessions perfectly. Ailsa gently guides her clients, giving them enough challenge(s) and new tools to move forward, and always wrapped up in empathy and compassion.

One of the reasons Ailsa manages this is because she has had her own struggles with societal expectations of bodies and appearances, and of how we manage our lives. In addition, mothering comes with its own challenges. It is the hardest job there is, especially when being done solo a great deal of the time. Ailsa expresses the joys and lows of mothering so well in her journal. Also, having her own daughters, Ailsa wanted to be able to model self-acceptance and compassion for them, to prevent her own and society's pain being transferred into their lives.

It was through her internal struggles with her body, trying new diets and surgeries, that she came to accept "the entire untidy package called Ailsa". Ailsa had to come to love and trust her humanness, her body, and her gorgeous spirit too! This journey of acceptance and growth is so wonderfully apparent in her journal. Through sharing her innermost thoughts, pain and internal conflict, Ailsa will unsettle you and challenge you at times. And she will offer valuable insights, which no doubt will play a valuable part in the reader's own transformation.

The book is written with bravery, compassion, love, and a genuine desire to help. I am very proud of Ailsa, and I love her present-life manifesto. She trusts her body, loves to move it, believes in and loves people, and it is evident that she believes in herself too. Ailsa has proudly accepted that she is "perfectly imperfect", and I have no doubt that she will inspire a whole movement to assist others to do the same.

Congratulations Ailsa, and yes, how far you have come. Thank you for sharing a part of yourself and your story so generously, and inspiring us with your love of life, your body, and your sassy self!

– Dr Cate Howell CF, OAM, CSM

INTRODUCTION

I started writing a personal, reflective blog when my daughter Lily was 10 months old, and I was about to have weight-loss surgery. At first, I simply wanted a private space to reflect on my life. I was convinced I was on the precipice of a monumental change. Little did I know, I'd already jumped from a great height and was stomping down the mountain of expectations about how my body and life 'should' look. I had begun to appreciate some of my imperfections as possible strengths, though my self-belief often wavered. I yearned for just one thing – for my daughter to grow up really loving herself. I didn't need a damn Lap Band for that. I was already showing her how.

I never intended on sharing my unfiltered journal entries with the world. My reflections were intensely private as I wrote about struggling with body image and weight, the joy and heartbreak of mothering, my profound loneliness, and questioning my identity and purpose. I sat up on our hill pouring my heart out as I longed for my husband to come home from his FIFO* (fly-in fly-out) work in the mining industry. During those five years of blogging, I only shared my blog posts with a handful of trusted readers/friends.

Some of my clients began asking me how I came to be more comfortable being 'perfectly imperfect'. Initially, I couldn't remember when I began to question and rebuke diet-culture, when I learnt to enjoy moving my body with joy rather than exercising because I felt I should, and when I began to embrace the perceived imperfections in my body and in my life. Then I re-read my blog. It became apparent that through my experiences and reflections I grew wiser, sassier, and less apologetic for my body, my mothering, my need for love and my desire to be accepted. By the end, I was beginning to almost dig the entire untidy package called Ailsa.

In hindsight, the seeds had been sown years earlier after meeting several influential mentors at key points in my life. One very important moment was when I was begging for yet another diet from a dietitian and was instead encouraged by the unassuming, yet remarkably progressive woman to read Dr Rick Kausman's book *If Not Dieting, Then What*. From that day, my paradigm began to shift as I realised there was an alternative to the never-ending fight to lose weight and be 'good enough'. I had been introduced to the worldwide movement Health At Every Size® (HAES®) and it made perfect sense to me.

Understandably though, after years of trying to be thinner, the seduction of weight-loss was still palpable. I was living in a body that was very much above my most comfortable weight, and I still felt I needed to apologise for the space it took up in the world. Regardless of the new knowledge I had about how diets had actually failed *me*, I was still lured into the idea that gastric surgery would change my life for the better.

Did it? No.

I lost weight, then gained, then lost, then gained and so on. In my present body I have been both larger and smaller. Gastric surgery and weight-loss have *not* been the key to my happiness. What has impacted me the most has been adding self-compassion and gratitude to my life. Sass jumped aboard too, and then I really began to embrace moving my body and adding more joyful behaviours, all the while capturing how I felt through writing.

During the time I wrote my blog I had several surgeries, another baby and I met my step-daughter for the first time. I often found myself solo-parenting as my husband was working away in the mining industry, and I began a Masters Degree in Counselling and Psychotherapy. My mental and physical health improved in those years, even through the many difficult times I faced. What carried me through all the ups and downs was acknowledging the tough stuff and then counting my blessings each day; that was what comforted me most, and still does to this day.

Looking back at my blog posts, my struggle to disengage with diet-culture is very evident as weight-loss was still my goal. The language I used in my posts may trigger someone who struggles with disordered eating. Please take care of your own heart whilst reading my raw posts about trying to obtain the mythical 'perfect weight and perfect life'. Often as I've re-read parts, I feel as if I'm looking at a car wreck and can't look away. Please trust that I was learning from my lessons along the way. I have ceased to give the scales power as I did back then, and I now own my imperfections. Today, the reality is that I still have my ups and downs; some days I really struggle with being kind to myself, and other days I am bursting with thanks and enthusiasm for my body and life. I am human and it's ok.

My posts may read as if I felt I needed to be thinner to provide better lessons for my children about body image, but I *do not* believe that. I wish for them to grow up being confident in their own bodies and to trust in their innate knowledge of what makes them feel well. May they rejoice in their strengths and own their individual sassiness! I wish for them to accept their 'imperfections', never feel ashamed, and love themselves madly. I hope they don't feel sadness about their bodies as I have felt in the past, but if they ever do, I will support them with all my heart.

I know that some stories I have shared may surprise and possibly unsettle people close to me. They are simply my version of what has occurred and impacted me; I know others' perspectives may be very different. I mean no harm. I just needed an outlet to reflect on why I struggle with who I am at times.

The blog posts were never intended on teaching anyone anything… except me!

Now I realise many of my underlying stories of not feeling 'good enough' and struggling with my changing identity speaks strongly to most women. I'm sharing my very private reflections in hope they are helpful as you explore your own stories of 'imperfection'.

You may be finding yourself knee deep in dirty nappies, dreaming of escape, or maybe you've skipped past that stage but still for the life of you, can't seem to like yourself enough even though you're an intelligent, capable woman! You are certainly not alone. I hope my book resonates with you and stirs something inside you to want more for yourself. I hope it makes you laugh, too, because life is far too serious and far too short. Be kinder to yourself and to others.

Much love and blessings, Ailsa x

By the way, my husband's name is Kent and my exercise machine is called Keith – yes, it may be confusing, but you'll get there.

Oh, and if you have an aversion to cussing, then some of my less articulate days may grate – be warned.

---

*Disordered eating: If you don't know much about what I mean please seek further knowledge. There is no way of telling by looking at a person if they struggle with disordered eating and/or they struggle with how their body looks. Often a person's suffering is dangerously hidden. Speaking about diets or weight in the public and private spaces you move in, regardless of your intentions, can inadvertently trigger disordered eating and mental anguish in others. The words you use **count**. Take care with what you say.*

** FIFO or fly-in fly-out, is a method of employing people in remote areas by flying them temporarily to the work site instead of relocating employees and their families permanently. It is often abbreviated to **FIFO** when referring to employment status. This is common in large mining regions in Australia.*

TIMELINE OF INFLUENCES

I was asked by a couple of readers where the insight for the strategies I use in the book came from. I believe the following moments in my life shaped me considerably, and they certainly give context to my reflections.

Studying Anthropology at the University of Adelaide – the realisation of perspective. There is no other, without self. Your life experience influences your point of view. There is no right or wrong opinion – simply perspectives. This turned my world upside down and helped me to catch myself and own my judgements of other people. It stops blame.

Studying Information Studies at Uni SA and working in the Commonwealth Carelink program – coming to the understanding that knowledge is power. Information can empower people and help change their lives.

Goddess Within workshop with Dianne McCann Mathews – I learnt more about my own power as a woman and that I was worthy of being loved and respected just as I was. The realisation of women's innate wisdom and that I already have the knowledge within me. To trust myself.

Self-development with Leonie Marks – the most profound yet simple pearl of wisdom Leonie gave me was: *"it's not your 'stuff'"*, as up until then, I took on board everyone else's opinion of me and owned 'their stuff' when it wasn't my burden to bear. We also worked on my perfectionist streak. Questioning my unrealistic expectations of myself and instilling the thought that I am good enough exactly as I am.

Health At Every Size® – when I was first introduced to the book *If Not Dieting, Then What?* by Dr Rick Kausman, my world was flipped upside down as I realised there was another, more compassionate side to understanding my body. I could begin to accept it as it is and then add more compassionate behaviours to my life to bring me more peace and joy. I also had a consult with Dr Kausman in Melbourne and he was a genuine, caring, progressive professional. I've continued to touch base with him over the years, and watched his progress in the field. I also had the privilege to attend his If Not Dieting Health Training with a group of fellow Adelaide-based health professionals; practice nurses, GPs, dietitians, psychologists, counsellors and psychotherapists. Once I completed my Masters degree, Dr Kausman referred my first HAES® psychotherapy client to me.

Birthing my daughters with my independent midwife, Marijke Eastaugh – I met Marijke through my work involvement with the Adelaide Hills Community Services Forum. When I finally fell pregnant with Lily (after IVF treatment) I knew I wanted an independent midwife to journey with me whilst pregnant, during birth, and to support us in the first few months after the baby was born. I learnt so much about the choices I had in the care that I required during those times. My midwife and my obstetrician had a history of working together, so I felt my care was complementary and the viewpoints balanced. Most importantly, I felt empowered by the knowledge I was gaining about my pregnancy and birth, and began to really understand that my body was not public property. I had a strong voice for both myself and my child. This was also the case when I had my second daughter, Tess. Through birth I was reborn as a mother and as an advocate for my body and my daughters' bodies. I became a Tigress Mother – fierce and protective.

Body empowerment – the concept that my body is not public property, that I have the right to choose how it is cared for and I have the right to have my boundaries respected was certainly evident through my surgeries and is still evident any time I am required to engage with health-care providers. I have been subjected to weight-shaming in the past, and I now know how to advocate for myself and others.

Studying Counselling and Psychotherapy at the University of Adelaide – intense self-reflection throughout my studies was absolutely necessary. It once again reinforced what I'd learnt in Anthropology – that it is imperative to check in on my own biases and point of view when trying to understand another person's perspective. I learnt that the main quality I wish to always have as a psychotherapist is humility.

2009

SO BEGINS THE CONTEMPLATION...

Self-absorbed in the nicest possible way

Today I embrace delving deep into my hopes and dreams whilst reflecting on how far I have come. Today, I'm not getting caught up in my daily list of jobs, instead I'm enjoying getting lost in my own thoughts.

But where has this all stemmed from?

Well, I am on another journey – another big one in my life.

I have decided to have gastric surgery – I will soon have a Lap Band. Wow. Writing that down is a step in itself, I can tell you!

I have been contemplating surgery for a couple of years, and now is the perfect time.

The time I am spending at home with Miss Lily – my 10-month-old baby girl – is the perfect time for me to get well again. To shed my excess weight and to stop the ticking time bombs that are no doubt going to go off in the future if I remain so overweight: diabetes, heart disease, joint problems etc.

I would like my daughter to grow up with an even more energetic, happy mother.

I want her to learn positive lessons about body image through my example and with my guidance.

The buck stops here. I will no longer damage myself, and I will do my damndest not to damage my daughter (knowingly of course).

Random thoughts pre-surgery

I have some thoughts and concerns of course; and here they are:

Can I do it with complete love for my body and trust in the Universe?

Why am I being led to this over and over if it is not meant to be for me?

Can I incorporate the very controlled medical side with an open, loving, spiritual mindset again, like I successfully did with IVF (in vitro fertilisation)?

Can I incorporate Dr Rick Kausman's *If Not Dieting, Then What®* philosophies with aspects that I have control over through the journey, such as listening to my body when full, eating what I crave, not counting calories, not judging food as good or bad, and not judging myself for my eating behaviours, moving more because I want to, eating food that makes my body feel well.

I am afraid that my love of food – an integral part of my life – will be affected, especially eating out.

If it doesn't work and I regain my weight, what extra psychological damage have I done to myself?

Is accepting that I need assistance with my weight/health, accepting myself?

Am I truly accepting myself exactly as I am? I do love my body for being strong, for my good skin and hair, and for my passion and sensuality – is that enough?

I love how far I have evolved in the past few years but am I dishonouring my body by willingly allowing it to be cut, altered and, in many ways, restricted? Will this restriction factor into other areas of my life, emotionally maybe?

What horrible aspects of being Banded will affect me? Big and small things?

Keith – my cross trainer

Well Keith and I are in love. It's an on-again off-again relationship, but right now we are very connected. Keith is my cross-training machine. I have named him 'Keith the Killer', and have been working out on him about five times a week. He was a 'vital' purchase two years ago and has been kindly drying my sheets until I recently put him into action.

I have also been doing weight exercises, stretches, abs, and working out on my dad's home gym and rowing machine – her name should be Barbara the Biatch (she is unforgiving). I go to my parents place twice a week, and my dad and I work out together while my mum looks after Miss Lily – it works well. Between those visits, I use Keith and my own weights at home. So far, I have kept to this schedule for approx. three months and although it is not showing on the scales, I am feeling much trimmer, fitter, and more flexible. I am also dead keen to get out more and move; whether it is collecting the wheelie bin from down our steep drive, to walking further with Lily in the pram. I am very motivated.

This can't be anything but good leading up to my surgery. I am proud of myself.

Kent and I – early days

What I have already manifested

It's always good to take stock.

In 2001/2, I had just finished my second degree, started a new job, come out of a destructive relationship, and was living with my parents, feeling miserable. I was smoking, drinking, and was pretty poor and overweight.

I had a summer of collecting myself and was dusting myself off when along came a boy – rather, a man – who seemed a tad too boring for me.

I initially pushed him away. Then one day it dawned on me to get off my high horse and look at what a genuine, lovely guy was in front of me. It was Kent. I fell in love, told him I loved him. He said he'd already loved me for a long time. It was magic.

Old patterns were still very much in play though – smoking, drinking, being Miss Right all the time. He was patient with me. He had his own personal struggles, including how he felt about having any more children and they played havoc with our future plans for a while.

One day I stopped and listened when he said, "but why does it have to be your way all the time?"

Yes, why indeed?

I started to drop my guard without losing any power. In fact, I gained so much from letting go – Kent too. And much further down the track he let go of some of his own fears as well. Wow, the relationship started to really work then.

I'd moved into his lovely house on the hill, and we bought puss-cats who made us swoon. We got engaged and then married soon after, having a wonderful celebration at home – a 'big party, little wedding'.

On our honeymoon we travelled to the USA for the first time together for an extended period. For four weeks we couldn't stop talking and having fun. We were in our own bubble. What a great friendship we have.

On our return, I quit smoking, and he had surgery so we could try and fall pregnant. We chilled out our social life and ticked along, working hard. At the end of 2006 we bought a business and set about getting that up and running while I still worked full-time at my job. We tried to fall pregnant, without success.

Throughout this time and for years prior, I had tried various diets with momentarily successful periods of weight-loss before eventually putting the weight (and then some) back on – usual story!

In 2007 we booked ourselves in for IVF in January 2008, as Kent's surgery hadn't been as successful as we'd hoped. First try failed – devastating. But then our second try worked and I had a wonderful pregnancy in 2008, giving birth to a gorgeous girl in late December of '08.

I had almost booked myself in for a Lap Band in 2008 before I fell pregnant, then the thought went out of my mind as I lost weight whilst pregnant. I listened to my body, ate smaller meals, and was treated for a thyroid condition.

We are nearly ten months into our new roles as Mummy and Daddy and loving it. She is divine. I thankfully won't return to any formal work for a while. I have a chance now to help with the business, be at home with my baby, look at what I want in life, and now to make myself *well* again!!

In 2001 I dreamt of a time where I didn't smoke, had my own home, had a wonderful partner/maybe even a husband, had a child, had a fulfilling career, didn't party all the time but still enjoyed a great social life, got on well with my family on my own terms and felt more at peace with myself. I have all that now. Another missing piece is to be well, slender, fit, and happy. To be a weight that is right for my frame, and to be damn healthy.

I think I am going to manifest this for myself next – wahoo!

I am truly blessed. xxx

Thank you, Universe. xxx

What goes up must come down

Equanimity is what I desire – the ability to perceive all aspects of my life with acceptance and patience, and to avoid extreme reactions.

At least I can understand what is occurring. I was oh so high for the past few days, to the point of a frenzy of positive emotions – I could barely concentrate on putting my socks on.

Last night, the black dog came and bit me hard. I was pulled into a pool of sadness.

As I allowed myself to ride the waves of grief, I promised myself to write about the feelings, as they are so important in my journey.

I read a few not-so-positive threads in a chat room about Banding. Some pretty sad stories from people struggling with their Lap Bands. Reality hit, and a ton of emotions came with it.

Anxiety: the sense of panic when I know I am about to start another 'diet'. They say it is not, but it will restrict me from eating what and all that I want. I cannot 'get off the diet' either; I am stuck with it unless I have further surgery to remove the Band. Basically, I am relinquishing control and that makes me feel claustrophobic. I can imagine having panic attacks just thinking about the foreign thing inside me.

Sadness: woe is me. Why do I have to keep enduring such awful things in my life due to my genetics? Looking back at my child within, I feel a sadness for her as she is again having to be poked and prodded and moulded into an acceptable shape. It's not fair. I don't really eat badly, maybe a little bit too much, but why do I have to be called obese – actually morbidly obese? I feel ok mostly, but then I look at myself in pictures and I wonder who that person is. It is not how I perceive myself.

Fear: if this doesn't work, how will I ever forgive myself? How much more psychological damage can I take? What will people think when they know I have been Banded? Fear of further shame.

I also fear that I have 'bluffed' my way into being given a Band. The doctors and dietitians I've seen have said I have come so far already by myself, and that I am a perfect candidate for a Band. I feel like I have given them the good side of my life – yes, I eat well, but sometimes I'll eat a meal of junk food you wouldn't believe!! Yes, I exercise regularly, but that comes and goes. I am on a 3-month Keith-bender right now, but what about in six-months' time?? Yes, I have read and followed Rick Kausman's book, but why am I then still overweight if I listen so well to my body? Surely it would have said: hey, only eat carrot sticks, as *damn* you've put on some kilos – lol! They seem to think I don't need to see the psychologist until after the surgery. Yeah, I'm ok (head jerking to one side), promise!! lol.

Thank god for a new day. Today, equanimity feels closer to the mark.

I thank the Universe for offering me both sides and allowing me to listen. I remember that all this knowledge is already mine, I just need to be open to it. And I am.

Some days are diamonds!

Wednesday, October 21, 2009 was a diamond. The day was warm, the sun was out, my mind was sharp, and I walked confidently – shoulders back, smile on my face to my first appointment at the clinic re: my Band.

I was bursting with enthusiasm and the right amount of control, so as not to seem too eager. I spoke at length about what I'd researched and my thoughts about how to make the Band work for me whilst incorporating my philosophies about being kind to myself.

It felt like a job interview and I got the position! I am to be fast-tracked along their medical appointments to get me Banded asap. Just a dietitian and surgeon appointment before my surgery is booked in – wahoo!!

In the back of my mind I am thinking about Xmas and New Year's Eve and how our travel plans will affect my ability to eat, as there are pre and post-op diet requirements.

Oh well, I endured a crap Xmas and New Year last year whilst waiting and then having Lily, then being in shock for the first two months – I can do hard! I can walk through fire and survive.

As Kent and I have discussed, there will always be something that comes up. Nothing like the present to start a new chapter in my life. I am chomping at the bit to see how my body will change.

Let's go!

Ego check

Just a note to self, Ms Ailsa: your ego seems to be a bit inflated in your last post.

Let enthusiasm not blanket reason.

Listen to those specialists that will have your life, and your body, in their control.

You must take each step with care and be sure to follow their instructions.

This isn't going to be a walk in the park, but it may well be life-changing if you make the journey with grace.

One foot in front of the other

I've broken up the next few weeks into mini-goals and contemplations. This week is to purely exercise every day, eat well and stop eating before I get overfull. So far, I have done just that and have made some gorgeous meals, including cold rolls and sushi today – yum.

I'm feeling very positive – more balanced than the highs and lows of last week.

It's a gorgeous night. The cool night air is lapping at me through the window screen. Very peaceful.

I'm enjoying myself as much as possible around Lily's routine. She began crawling yesterday, so I'm having to be quicker on my feet than before as she explores the house.

I felt blessed last night: Lily was a little restless. I went in and picked her up from the cot. She stopped crying the minute I had her against me and quickly fell asleep in my arms. It was beautiful. Rather than get upset that my sleep was broken, I just treasured her little warm body against mine, her sweet breath on my chest. She'll be all grown up before I know it, so moments like those are gold.

That is what counts in life.

Let me never forget. xx

Feeling loved

I have had moments in the last few days I feel I need to acknowledge for being wonderful and completely separate to my body-image issues. I spent a wonderful few hours with a bunch of girlfriends over the weekend and came away feeling buoyed with love and friendship.

These women love me for me, not how much I weigh; and I feel exactly the same way about them. I am, however, looking forward to going to a spring race in the future with them and being able to wear a pretty, off-the-shelf frock. I am looking forward to not standing out physically in a group of my friends – unless of course it's because of my height!

The other moment was my darling husband returning home after being away for three days. When he hugged me, I felt smaller already and wondered how different it will feel when we can embrace and be closer to each other once I shed some weight.

Cuddly is good, yes, but being able to receive a big, *long* bear hug from him will be amazing.

Mindset

I often feel that I have already been Banded. My mind is so set on a new existence to a certain degree, that I forget I haven't had the op yet. Odd, huh? I suppose I am already exercising more and incorporating moving into every day. I am being conscious of my food-portion sizes and I am particularly listening to what my body is telling me.

I am also thinking differently about myself – probably the strangest thing. I forget that I haven't lost weight yet, but inside my head, I already have. When reality does set in and I get conscious of how I look, I tell myself that it is just temporary and then put on a huge smile and walk tall. I remind myself to enjoy the present and to appreciate the magic moments in every day. Life is too short to focus wholly on body image – *I am a perfect soul in an imperfect body.*

Quiet contemplation

Well I'm back after meeting the surgeon and I am feeling somewhat stumped. My feelings of excitement soon dissipated the minute he started talking. He was extremely efficient and provided all the information he was required to give, but his manner was typical of a busy medico – not very warm.

Hey, I wasn't expecting hugs but maybe a little more enthusiasm? He did state that he was purely there to help me achieve a better level of health, not a particular weight-loss, lifestyle etc.

Thankfully, my experience with other medical professionals such as the IVF specialist, and even the team of doctors and nurses who delivered Miss Lily has shown me that I don't necessarily need to be close to them to have wonderful outcomes. Think I'm just spoilt in some of the people I do have in my life that assist me with my health and make me feel... well, loved, I guess. Those friendships have and do lift me to wonderful heights when I call on their help. The meeting today is just a means to an end. In the past I probably would have backed out, but today I realise that he is not the one who is going to change my life – *I am*.

Apart from all of that, I have a date booked: Wednesday, 13 January, 2010.

So now what??

Well, first is the seven weeks leading up to Xmas – hot weather, Xmas parties and a few extra parties on top. Best I keep up the exercise first thing in the cool of the morning! Eat without getting overfull, drink lots of water, and have FUN!

I've been putting off buying any new clothes, but I just might go out and buy a pretty skirt to cheer me up for the silly season.

Speaking of fun, ...here's my brother, Nick, his gorgeous partner, Cat, and our Aunty Jill laughing at Miss Lily's antics

I wonder what will surface

I woke this morning after looking through photos last night and wondered what was going to surface for me emotionally as I lose weight.

I feel that when I moved to Queensland when I was 20, and began to over-eat, I started my journey to the excess weight I carry now. But is that really it?

As I look through photos of my life, I see a girl who has always been conscious of her weight and felt 'too big' (by whose standards, I don't know!).

I also see a girl at a whole range of weights having a ball with such a wide variety of friends over the years. Some of the photos include old flames, and this is where it gets a bit interesting.

Obviously, body image is intrinsically caught up with sexuality. I have feelings of shame about myself. The power my body had was a force I often abused, I think. I didn't value myself enough to only accept relationships with men who really cared for me.

When I was my thinnest, I was in a destructive relationship and felt completely ashamed and unloved. After that relationship ended, I moved to Queensland

and started to put on weight. I then met a lovely guy who did care for and love me for me, even though I was heavier than I'd ever been. That pattern continued until this point where I am at my happiest in my relationship with my husband but I have also been my heaviest in the relationship. Weird, huh?!

Hmmm, does this also stem from my relationship with my father whom I adore and who I was very close to until I became a young pubescent woman? From about the age of 13 on he didn't treat me the same. I remember at that stage I was craving his attention, but it wasn't there. Maybe that's why I then focussed my attention on boys.

We are close again now, but somehow I feel less sexualised in this overweight body so I think he can look at me without being uncomfortable in my sexual presence. Does that make sense? I think so, but wow, what a revelation!

Also, at around the age of 12, my mother started including me on her diets – calorie counting and the scrutiny of my body went from there. This along with puberty probably buggered up how I felt about my body image.

I wonder how this will go as each kilo comes off. Who will be affected by it apart from me?

My mother? My father?

We will see, I am sure.

Thanks to my body

I have been thinking a lot about my body, and thinking loving thoughts about where it has brought me so far. So I give thanks to it, just as it is now – 'warts' and all.

Thanks to my body for:

- Being strong and tall
- Carrying my beautiful daughter and birthing her safely
- Healing quickly after Lily's birth
- Feeding Lily and helping her grow into her gorgeous self
- Being full and sexy
- Playing a damn good game of netball
- Being coordinated at sport
- Being able to boogie all day/night
- Enjoying working out on Keith
- Being able to swim like a dolphin
- Having lovely skin, hair, and eyes
- Being healthy and vibrant
- Getting me through 30-odd amazing years

I'm now prepared to let go of my body's present form and look forward to more things to give thanks for that will arise on my journey!

Lily and I in 2010

2010

BODY CHANGES / FIFO / SURPRISE / SICK

Silly season has passed

The silly season has passed without too much drama and fuss – just lots of nice family get-togethers and a few road trips. Kent, Lily, and I have had a lovely two weeks together; the only thing missing was some one-on-one time with my husband, but you get that when you have a one year old! Yes, she turned one. Kent and I had tears of joy and gratitude on Xmas day and her birthday. Yay! We made it, and she's simply divine!

Throughout these last few weeks I've of course been thinking about the op and the pre and post-op diets. This has led to a bit of anxiety for me around meals. What should I have before I can 'no longer eat it'? I have done a little bit of emotional eating because of this, but I have also reminded myself that, to quote Rick Kausman: "I can have it if I really want it, but is it really what I feel like eating"?

Once I said that to myself, I was often content with a normal meal rather than steak, pizza, and fluffy white bread – 'just in case I can never eat it again'. Anyway, I realised I was trying to remove the emphasis on food all the time – it's just food – when I should be enjoying the rest of the holiday. Sun, ocean, family, friends!

I'm pleased I have already done some great work around the psychology of my relationship with food and my body, because it's so easy to get into the diet cycle. I have started my pre-op diet today and I am already obsessing with what I'm going to eat next because I feel the deprivation of a very low-calorie diet. My feelings of hunger and satiety are all over the place because my head-hunger is winning over my body-hunger.

Diets are definitely EVIL. This is purely needing to happen to shrink my liver for the op as they need to move it when placing the Band. I have 10 more days. I keep telling myself that it is ultimately for my daughter, so she has a healthy mummy. I will endure it, and *this too shall pass.*

Surprisingly doing a.o.k

Well, I'm about to finish day five of my pre-op diet and I am feeling fine. I know, though, that if this diet was supposed to be long term I'd have had a big ol' pizza and a block of choc by now, worrying about being deprived.

Keith (the cross trainer) and I have renewed our relationship and I have managed to better my distance every day. I'm also doing some weights to try and sort my arms out, and so I can lift my big bubba!!

I am in an extra-efficient mood leading up to the op – organising everything within an inch of its life and then making lists about everything once, twice, and maybe three times over. It's satisfying. I'm happy and excited about next Wednesday. Also looking forward to the down-time post-op where I might sleep some extra hours and read.

I'm not afraid of complications with the surgery, but I am realistic and realise they could occur. I have therefore updated my funeral wishes and made a list of 'just in case' stuff. I know it scared Kent, but it is simply life.

Well, off the sad stuff – told you I was organising everything in my life! A girl has to think she has some things in control... ba ha ha!! As if!

The Universe will always decide.

Blessings and good night.

All is quiet in the house

It's 40-something degrees outside, but in this lovely air-conditioned home it's about 23 and the family are having a cat nap. I've woken before daddy and daughter and am happily tapping away whilst having a miso soup. Kent and I are off for a romantic dinner tonight and it's Lily's 1st birthday party Sunday. Aah... the girl has woken – little giggles coming from her room, *cute*.

I am still conscious of shrinking my liver enough to perform the op safely. I am willing the little bugger to rapidly shrink, even with a splash of champers, a portion of cake and a smear too much butter here and there in the equation. I believe in it – the Universe will provide.

Lily, Kent and I at Lily's 1st bday

One more sleep

Only one more sleep. I am STARVING today. Think it's my body 'coming down' from the champers and nibbles on Sunday at Lily's party. My in-laws have arrived to care for her and help with the business. I want some peace before tomorrow, but the house is full of people. In a perfect world I would like some time alone to watch a movie and eat some pizza and chocolate. Instead, I will have veggies and an early night with my book if possible. Am I scared? No. How do I feel? A bit ashamed. Why? Because I have got myself into this situation and now I am having to have an operation to fix it.

My mother has just looked at me (yes, she's here too) with a mix of loathing and distrust – well that's what it looked like to me. I think she loathes the fact that her daughter is having one of 'those' sorts of operations. Distrust? Well, I think she doesn't trust my opinion or that of the doctor and specialists that this op is for me.

One positive is she'll at least keep it quiet because she doesn't want to highlight her daughter's 'weaknesses'. I just need people around me that love and care for me and that will bring positive energy into my space. It's not me; I know it's her stuff. I'm just a bit fragile, so I'll take care of myself and keep some distance.

Home and full of wind!

I'm home – yay! Missed my baby girl soooo much! Though she's been perfectly fine being doted on by her Nan and Pop.

The op is a success so far. I am feeling pretty lousy due to the amount of built-up wind in my tummy. I am supposed to be resting, but it's not easy when the house is full of people and everyone is doing stuff – makes me feel guilty just lying about.

My mum has been good to me (after my previous post). Before the op, she rang to tell me that she loved me then came and saw me straight after I got out of theatre. I know she loves me, she is just smitten with Lily and all her attention goes to her. She sent me a text after the op saying she loves me as much as Lily. Odd, I know. Oh well.

Apart from fleeting moments when I think: *What have I done to myself? Why have I put myself into so much pain? What if I can't eat anything I like again?* I am pretty happy. I know that *this too shall* pass.

Stuck in my head

I have been feeling a bit miserable the last few days. I am completely stuck in my own thoughts and am furiously beating myself up – ah, self-sabotage, it's such a familiar feeling. I have lost weight, gone through a nasty op, I'm still tender at times and am only two weeks out of hospital but do you think I can give myself a break??

I am cross that I'm making some not-so-great food choices at times, yet I am sticking to smaller meals. I have been cranky (sorry Kent) and 'stuff' is coming up. I want to be slim immediately and wonder why my arse hasn't fallen off and been replaced with Elle Macpherson's because hey, I've been working pretty hard at this for all of four weeks! Ha, ha!

At least I can see what is going on – can't drag myself out of it just yet – but it is obvious that as the weight has fallen away, 'stuff' is coming up. I won't fight it, I'll just try and be a bit kinder to myself.

It could also be the fact that I haven't had chocolate for a few days. Maybe my body is in shock! I'm on the right path though.

I am going to be fit and slender soon. xx

Change

Funny how you can beat yourself up for feeling anxious and upset without taking into account what is happening in your world.

Mine is changing – rapidly! Lily is starting childcare tomorrow. My mother will have her every Thursday and that means I am officially working with my husband in our business.

I am feeling sad for leaving Lily at childcare and sad that our first special year together as mummy and baby has ended. I may never have that first year with a baby again (getting teary now). I am now going to have to find the energy to put into the business and still be a mum. I am struggling already. I am also going to be working in an industry that doesn't interest me really at all. I am doing it for love and for our family to prosper. I am afraid that my identity will really fade away by being on call for Kent regarding work and then on call for Lily every other moment.

The only thing I have control over really is my weight-loss and my physical change. I'll have to remember not to let that aspect get manic. I'll have to find moments in my days/weeks/months when I am just 'me' – though she is a little faded at the moment; I don't know who she is.

Oh, I am sad – maybe mourning the passing of a chapter in my life?

My earning potential is basically zip at the moment too. I am bringing in nothing and feeling kept – it's horrible. Money woes taint my relationship with Kent. He works too much and doesn't ever switch off work even when he is home. As a couple, we are distant. I feel invisible to him.

We are generally kind to each other and enjoy being together with Lily, but the mad passion of our early days has wound back. I know it's very normal, but I hate it.

I'm really spilling it out today. Lucky this is a private blog.

I type with damp hands that are wiping away my tears.

Change is happening.

Hold on.

Trust.

Pretty good after my last emotional purge

My last post purge was just what I needed. I've been feeling a bit better. Kent and I talked and had lots of big hugs. I am still experiencing the same feelings, but the last couple of days working with him have made me feel a little excited. Excited by the prospect of spending time with him away from our roles as mum and dad, and excited by how I might be able to really contribute to 'the cause', our business, and to our finances.

Lily has adjusted beautifully to her new world at childcare. I must remember that she is her own person and I can't control every part of her world – I am just here to watch over and care for her. She is an autonomous being, learning and growing in her own right. She amazes me every day. I am in awe of her intellect, her humour, and her curiosity.

I know it is up to me to not feel 'invisible' too. As a mum, I am always in the background when I'm with Lily. That's ok though, I feel like I am working in the background on my physical self and one day I'll fly.

I am also working (or really just dreaming) of who I'll become in the sense of my career. I am in no hurry to have any answers to 'what will I be when I grow up?' I am just happy to let the Universe show me. I am watching, listening and learning. I am blessed to not have to proceed with this metamorphosis whilst having to work in my old job as well as being a mum. Thankfully, that space is there for me now, no matter how poor it is making us at the moment.

Me, me, me!

I type this as Lily is crying up a storm in her bed. A ½-hr sleep this morning is NOT enough baby girl. Got to read more of my parents' guide book to toddlers – she's pushing my buttons!!! Urgh.

Back home from cleaning the workshop office; now it will be lovely for me to work in.

Order = Calm = Productivity = Prosperity!

I've realised driving along that I am in urgent need of some 'me' time. Not 'me' time where I go off with the girls and drink far too much and then feel crap and miserable the next day; 'me' time where I can workshop ideas and passions and create time and things that make me happy.

I have been creating a dream vision board.

I made one a few years ago but I wanted to make a more up-to-date one.

My dream board ended up being about turning into a FOX and enjoying being fit, becoming wealthy and having glamorous moments and objects. On the other hand, being thrifty and enjoying all that is lovely about being at home – home-grown veggies, nice areas at home for relaxing (future pool), and socialising, cooking with Lily, lounging in a luxurious boudoir...

And love of course. I always wish for more love. xx

I had a lovely time putting it together yesterday. Actually, yesterday was a good day. Kent and I cleaned the house in the morning, and I registered to play netball this season and all the girls seemed excited to have me back. It will be great exercise and some great 'me' time too.

Lily had fun and cuddles with the netball girls and kids. It will be another great community for her to be a part of as she grows up.

By the way, The Lily Monster stopped protesting about 10 minutes ago and is sound asleep.

1 to Mummy! Yeah!

Tick of approval

I met with my dietitian today – my first post-op appointment at the clinic. I'm just learning about my new body signals with this Band and it is up to me to decide if I want any 'fill'* in my Band or not. She suggested that if I have too much fill and can't eat foods that I love, that maybe I should get some taken out, as lifestyle is very important.

I agree; food is a passion for me. On the other hand, though, I had this op to move some weight, so if the weight-loss stops then I'll have to consider a fill. Right now, I'm going to keep up my exercise and keep to my small portion serves and listen to my body, then we can see what the scales say.

I am still dropping weight, slightly I think. I have my first appointment with the specialist GP at the clinic in two weeks' time where we'll discuss getting a fill or not.

I'm open-minded right now.

Answers will come to me, I'm sure.

The Lap-band is a piece of plastic, and on the inside of it is a balloon. The balloon can be filled with saline (salt water) and this causes the balloon to expand. The band is filled incrementally to allow a person to eat smaller amounts of food, and be satisfied for some period of time.

Excited!

So I don't believe that BMI is a true indication of a person's health, but I thought I'd whack my digits into a BMI calculator just to see if anything had changed. Well, yes it has! It is a little win for me; not that I let BMI really phase me because I am a tall, large-boned goddess. I will not be boxed into a 'category' unless it is the damn fine, strong, goddess with a kind heart and curvylicious body category! Ha ha!

I am loving Keith almost daily, and the other days I'm swimming with Lil and just trying to be more active.

I am eating well and enjoying a whole range of lovely foods in reasonably small serves (but not tiny). Surprisingly, this last week, my mother and I have had a couple of decent conversations about diets etc., and she has even complimented me on my mental progress with Rick Kausman's philosophies.

I was sceptical because all my grown life she has made me read book after book on diet/health. I can think of at least 12 different books I have succumbed to, and it has not made a speck of difference to my health, just made me feel more miserable and a failure at losing weight.

BOO to those books and BOO to my mother!!!

Grrr, just felt extremely angry for a minute.

Hmmm.

Down

It's been a miserable day.

I'm ok with it, and understand that some days I'm just going to be a bit blue.

I am tired. Really, really tired. I think it's a combo of working my butt off on Keith daily (but not today), chasing after Lily, and feeling anxious about general 'change'. I also feel nauseated today; not sure why. Haven't eaten anything odd, just feel blurgh. I've had toast and a tea for dinner, and now I think I'll head to bed. The sun is still up, but I don't care.

"Tomorrow, tomorrow, I love you tomorrow... you're only a day away..." Thanks Annie, I'll take your advice.

P.S. Checking my weight daily (tut, tut) and it is not dropping by miles, so I am a bit down. I know better. Really I do.

I'll be kinder on myself tomorrow. Promise.

Swimming in the morning – water therapy.

Night, night. xx

Feeling insightful

The doldrums have passed. I am well again (and not pregnant – all that nausea had me worried for a moment!).

After all my worry about the scales, I weighed in lighter the next day – what the...????

From what I can see on the Band chat rooms, most people are crying out for fills in their Bands as they feel hungry and are not seeing the weight-loss they want. I think some of them may be trapped in feelings of deprivation – which makes you feel hungry, no matter what. I don't want that. I want instead to forget about food, to remove the focus on it.

My food journaling is getting less and less frequent. I don't feel as concerned that if I don't write down everything I eat, something (like a biscuit) might pass me by and sneak up and leap onto my thighs! I'm doing well. I am eating great food and enjoying myself.

I am LETTING GO!!

Wonder what the response will be from the GP? I think it may be very positive.

Getting back to the nausea. I think it had a lot to do with some 'stuff' coming up as I've shed more weight. Kent and I have chatted, which was great for me to vocalise some of my thoughts. Thin was not so safe for me all those years ago – from the age of about 15; when I was thin I was sexually objectified by boys and men (aren't we all?!). I allowed them to make comments about my body and often encouraged the attention, but deep down I was sickened by it. When I think back, I have feelings of shame, guilt, hurt, and a longing for real love.

I've had several comments from some of my female friends about my weight-loss, and I have felt shock and fear that they have 'seen' me. Part of it is the stigma about the Band (I am sure I will keep it to myself), but a lot of it, I think, is people seeing the person I am underneath.

I feel I have shielded myself from attention with my weight. I am confident that people who love me now, love me for my mind and spirit. I love myself now, too, and am so much more confident in my intellect and emotional maturity than the thin girl I was years ago. She sort of knew she was ok, but was very tangled.

I am now me and free.

So maybe the nausea is fear; fear of being thin.

This is what I am working on. I think I'll be ok.

Insightful huh?! Blessings...

P.S. Thanks for listening to me. xxx

Doubt is an evil, evil thing

Yesterday I had an amazing two appointments with my specialist GP and the exercise physiologist. They were both very, very happy with my progress and congratulated me several times. I was elated after seeing them, but now an element of self-doubt has crept back in – dammit!!

I'm a bit concerned that I am being a bit anti-fill, and will set myself up for disappointment if I do need some fill. Oh how crazy can one's mind be?!!! That's why I had the op – for restriction – der!!

Anyway, I then went and met the exercise physiologist and he was very happy to hear about Keith, and that I use weights and do ab exercises, swim, and am playing netball this season. In fact, he thought the only way was up for me seeing that I'll increase my exercise. He said I seem motivated and that I have always been an active person, so I will just keep getting more and more active. Wahoo! That's exactly how I feel.

He also popped me onto a stationary bike so I could do a mini fitness test, and then I can do one again in six months to see how much fitter I am. He was impressed with my fitness level, and kept putting the resistance up to raise my heart rate, as it wasn't pushing me enough! Te he.

Love you, Keith! Mwah, mwah!

After the physiologist's advice, I'm going to invest in a fit ball and a heart-rate monitor – look out! Ha ha.

As you can see, the exercise part pumps me up, so I was all happy and then...

Bloody self-doubt creeps in (with the *Jaws* theme playing in the background – *daa-dum...*)

It's saying: what if you stop losing weight in the next four weeks? *Daa-dum...*

Are you just being stubborn about the fill when you really need it?

Daa-dum...

Maybe your portion sizes are really too big?

Daa-dum... daa-dum...

You are eating lots of fruit and veg now, but will it last?

Daa-dum... daa-dum...

Am I kidding myself that I'll ever really be slender?

Daa-dum... daa-dum...

HELLLLOOOOOOOO – where is my positive mindset?

Daa-dum... daa-dum...

Bugger this.

P.S. To my mind: I am lighter than I was the 1st of Jan. It is my four-year wedding anniversary today. My husband loves me fat or thin, and I love him to death for that and everything else about him. We are going to have a great candle-lit meal tonight that I'm cooking especially, and I am starting to feel a bit more foxy.

Back off bad thoughts!!!

Summing up my life

Having our four-year wedding anniversary on Thursday made me do some reflecting. I looked at my life and how it is right now.

I have to say that I have manifested so much of my dream lifestyle already.

I am not 'working' as such, I am spending time at home, organising and planning.

I am exercising daily and moving throughout my day rather than being stuck at a desk.

I am focusing on my health and eating wonderful, fresh, vibrant foods and feeling WELL.

I am raising a gorgeous daughter, and am able to give her cuddles and smooches any time.

I am married to my amazing friend and partner, and live in a beautiful home with a view to die for (and with two lovely puss-cats too).

All in all, the only thing missing is for Kent to feel that his life is what he always dreamt it to be. I wish him more time for himself and with the family, and I wish us abundance so we don't feel the stress of finances.

I know it is coming.

I can FEEL it in every cell of my body.

Our wedding day

Time can be fluid

I truly believe that time is not constant. Sometimes it stretches and sometimes it simply disappears. I always hope for a bit of a stretch if I am running late for something, and often it happens, and I end up on time.

This last week, time has been slowing it seems – waiting for an event. My watch stopped, the clock in the shed also stopped. So my sense of time has been, well... off, so to speak. I haven't felt the need to pick up Lily's toys two or three times a day. I haven't felt the need to take a clean load out of the washing machine since Friday. Dishes are gathering, paperwork nesting all around crannies in the house. All in wait for the news that was about to be delivered...

Yesterday, our present and future collided. We are again on a new path – business and life wise. Kent will close his business and start working again in the mining industry. I will be a 'single mum' while he is away for possibly weeks at a time. He will fly-in and fly-out (FIFO) for the next six months... ish, and then be based in Adelaide. We will be able to pay off some debt and live more comfortably.

We hope that time will be good to Kent, too, and will provide him more leisure time than he has now. We will desperately miss each other while he is away. My heart breaks thinking about it, but the timing is divine. We will endure the tough bits and revel in the joyful parts.

Time to buy some new batteries for the clocks that have stopped. Life is moving on and time is on our side.

Best I go hang out that washing.

sweaty after a workout

One big, glittery gold star!

Ok, thanks to a lovely friend Leonie's suggestion, I am awarding myself a big, fat, glittery gold star for all of my progress!

I sit here with a towel around my neck to stop the beads of sweat from hitting the keyboard, my arms are comfortably aching, and my breath is just getting back to normal after a great workout – my third since Monday.

I am loving all the energy I have, and how my body loves all this physical activity. Now, to get off this damn 'puter and onto cleaning and organising the house before I have to pick Miss Lily up from my folks.

Ciao for now, and Blessings to the Universe for helping me to reach my dreams!!

Mwah! xxx

Sick

It's hard to stay focussed and positive when a flood is happening in your nose. Thanks to Lily we are all now sick with colds. Amazing how we can all love each other just as much when we are all crusty and sick... Lily has been so cute at times with her runny nose and little cough.

We had a good weekend, just the three of us hanging out together at home and getting some jobs done. My focus is on trying to get my paperwork/things organised so I can feel a level of safety in the midst of all this change.

With this cold, the Universe has dealt me a reminder to slow down and LET GO. I can't focus on anything, so I may as well rest and sleep when I can.

It's hard to stay positive about my weight-loss progress because my mind is playing with me while I am not feeling 100%.- *Maybe your weight-loss will slow completely or even stop and you'll gain weight again?* Blasted bad thoughts.

I don't have an appetite for anything normal, but chocolate and toast could easily carry me through. :P

It's the Year of the Tiger this year, which is my Chinese symbol, too. The Tiger is a sign for bravery. I think this year is one where I'll have to be brave. I am not afraid of the challenge, but I can see that it is going to be tough.

I will draw strength from the Universe and trust.

FIFO (again)

Kent has been gone now for almost two weeks and we have missed him terribly, but life has gone on and Lily has been beautiful company for me. We've had lots of extra cuddles together – so cute! I suppose the everyday routine I have with Lily has kept my mind off missing Kent. If I get upset I just imagine that he is just at the workshop working, not thousands of kms away and I feel better.

I think I have a new level of emotional maturity that I obviously didn't have when he worked away prior to our marriage. Back then I bitched and whinged all the time about him being apart from me. These days, I have waves of sadness when I ache for him, but then I tell myself that *this too shall pass*, and that it is ok to be sad, but just trust that the time is right and that the Universe wants me to use this time as positively as possible. So that's what I am trying to do. Rejoice in everyday small joys, like right now I can feel the warmth of the sun bathing me through the window. It's like a gentle embrace. I give thanks for being able to acknowledge the beauty in my days.

I have two white-bandaged big toes right now. I've had issues with ingrown toenails and decided to get them fixed properly so I can get back into my sneakers and stop working out in thongs (how is that for committed?!).

I had the op yesterday; the edges of the nails shouldn't grow back now. It wasn't too painful. I just feared the procedure because when I was about 16 I had months of horrid ops and infected toes. Interesting that they've become a problem again. More 'stuff' coming up I wonder, or simply because I'm on my feet now after a sedentary job for eight years? Who knows.

A bit shocked

I've just pulled out a few of the dieting paraphernalia I have kept from the past 10 years and looked up how much I weighed at the beginning of the diets, and how much I lost. I've already surpassed the last 10 years of diet losses and am now in foreign weight-loss country – wow!

I am feeling a little anxious about the unknown aspect of being thinner than I have been the last 10 years, because often it is easier to gauge yourself by what weight you were at different points in your life.

I am now definitely going to be lighter than I was in my past two relationships and am heading back into Uni-weight days now... then I'll cross back into the 'living in Qld days' and that's where I put most of my weight on. After that, well, I am in a very long, lost land of teenage dieting years. Far out!!

It actually feels obtainable now, and without all the angst that has come with horrible diets where I am forever berating myself for being 'bad' and promising myself the world if I am 'good'. Deprivation to gorging and back again. That can bloody well stay in my past!

I am loving Keith and loving eating well. It is a whole different mind-set.

I am also kind to myself, and understand that some days I am hungrier than others and some days I will eat 'occasional' foods and enjoy them!

How liberating!

So, although the numbers are still a factor to see how my weight-loss progresses, they no longer define me because now I am in an unknown land – it's new and colourful and loving.

It's raining tears

Kent left this morning at 4am. Lily cried as he left. I'm very sad this time. Going to have to pull myself out of the feelings of loss. It's raining here, like the sky is crying for Lily and I knowing that we're missing him already.

Chin up, chicken.

This too shall pass. xx

Psych squiggles

I just remembered that I had my first appointment with the psychologist from the Band clinic a few weeks ago. He was nice enough, but I didn't get a lot out of the session except that he thinks I have a great mind-set for success with the Band.

He drew a whole lot of diagrams and squiggles about how some people think their Bands are going to 'teach' them to 'be good' and those people quite often don't have successful long-term weight-loss. My approach: eating healthy, solid meals in smaller portions is what generally makes for success.

Ok, good. So I think I already knew that. :/

He did give me something to think about, though, when I spoke of the shame of having surgery and opting for the so called 'easy way out'. He said if it is an easy way out (which it isn't), why wouldn't people who care for me want me to lose my weight easily? Um yeah... why wouldn't they?? So ultimately it gets put back on the person that may judge me, as being their stuff – not mine. Brilliant!

Apart from that, I think our first appointment was ok, but I have barely warmed to him; and he has tough competition when I feel that I have worked on heaps of this already in previous heart-felt therapy with the divine Ms Leonie. xx

Zip

I have done zip for about 36 hours as I have a cold. I am still in my nightie and Lily has had the run of the house since yesterday morning. I now have dining room chairs in the lounge, and toys strewn across two rooms thanks to her nifty organisation – basically moving stuff all over the house. She is blocked from going into the kitchen or laundry area by gates, so she 'posts' items through the bars – cute.

She has also worked out how to turn the tv off at the switch and loves to pull at every cord in sight: computer, fax, tv, etc. I've been barely able to stop her. I just keep putting obstacles in her path to deter her, and she moves them or climbs over. Clever girl.

Occasionally, all is quiet and I look up and she's planted herself on one of the lounge chairs often with a teddy or doll under her arm while she watches tv. Sometimes Ned the cat also sits on her lap for cuddles.

I feel that I am ignoring her, but she just keeps on doing her own thing and coming up to me with 'gifts' from time to time or for cuddles when she wants one. I think she's a.o.k.

I have been immersed online.

I think having the Internet down for two weeks made me do more things; now I am back hooked to online information.

The thing I am really hooked on at the moment is a blog by a girl in the USA who has had a Lap Band. She is hilarious and inspiring. Her humour is right up my alley and makes me think that maybe I should open my blog to the world as she bravely does, but then again, I like my privacy right now and feel that I can say anything in my blog. Also, I am happy to use it as a tool for journaling (is that a word??). I feel more comfortable just jotting things down for me, and then when in public divulging snippets of info I am comfortable disclosing at the time.

My little buddy

I noticed yesterday in the supermarket that I talk a lot to Lil; I felt like a bit of a mad woman appearing to talk to myself as I whizzed around with the trolley, but again I think it is what you get for spending a lot of time alone with just a toddler for company!

Here's today's funny. She's been trying to put her own bibs on and knows where the clean ones are drying on the clothes horse. Well, she came around the corner this morning wearing a pair of my granny-knickers instead of a bib, and looking very pleased with herself! She looked puzzled when I burst out laughing.

Oh my little, funny love! xx

Lily and I

Workout world

So here is a documentation of the exercise part of my journey at present. Three months post-op:

I am LOVING my workouts! What the...?? Yes, I know, but I feel sooooo good after I do them.

At present this is my thang:

35 minutes on Keith the Killer cross trainer.

Lunges around the shed (Kent says I look like I am curtsying – "how do you do?").

Weights whilst sitting on my fit ball, then ab crunches on the ball and sets of exercises from my fitball workout DVD.

I am trying to do it four times a week.

Fridays I swim with Lily at her swimming class. Well, I hold her, bob around and avoid her splashes for 30 minutes, which I say is a form of exercise!

Saturdays I will be playing netball and training on a Wednesday night as often as possible with Kent away.

How's that for moving my bod? You GO GIRL!!!!

Clearly endorphins are obviously still pumping around my body after this morning's workout. Ha ha!

Back in my 20s

I've been thinking a lot about being in my 20s. I am feeling a little anxious when I look in the mirror at times, as this was my weight when I was about 23. I had just got back from living in Qld, where I'd packed on a heap of weight. I was miserable and feeling very uncool in ill-fitting clothes (often men's jeans etc., because that's all I could fit in). I also had a run of being boyfriend-less and lonely.

I have to say I had five damn shitty years. I made it through Uni and met tons of friends, but I wasn't really happy. In hindsight, I suppose it was my first decade of being really big. Before then I had been overweight, but it didn't really affect my confidence.

I know that it seems odd looking at myself now – way lighter than when

I was trying to fall pregnant and feeling uncomfortable with what I saw. I suppose that 23-year-old sad girl is just a memory.

More 'stuff' is coming up. I will take it as a sign to take stock of how far I have come. That uneasy feeling in my tummy is no longer there. I am in a very happy place – almost to the point of child-like happiness.

I feel free and loved, and I love myself just as I am.

Blessings my friends. xx

Attachment and giving thanks

I had a mini-meltdown at Kent Monday night. It was his first full day with us and he was so distant that he may as well have not been home. In his defence, he is battling a chronic cold, and he's been working 13-hour shifts for 13 days – but still, I was not impressed (nasty wifey, I know).

I cried in bed next to him as it all hit me that I have actually underestimated how this new line of work is going to affect us. I am alone for weeks at a time with Lily, which is hard. I then think that when Kent gets home he'll give me a break and all will be roses because all my needs will be met.

Well of course, my expectations are very high and don't take into account what he needs (rest, some time to finish packing up the workshop, just some time to do stuff he can't for the two weeks he is at work etc.).

Amongst my tears I knew that I was being too attached; I was relying on him to tend to my needs without considering how I can do that myself. I also gave myself a bit of a break because I'm pre-menstrual.

One thing that did hit me was that through all the years we had the business, even though I wasn't there working with Kent daily, I was a part of it and we talked about all aspects of it. Now, I don't have any knowledge of what he is doing, so I am cut off from that part of his life and we can't share as much anymore.

I feel that sometimes my life details bore him as they are very mundane. Then again, is that the usual thing stay-at-home mums feel? A bit insignificant compared to the 'real working world'?

I still feel very grateful every day to be home and living a happy life, albeit without my husband. But he'll be finished this job in June sometime hopefully – not much longer.

Blessed

Yesterday was another diamond day.

Lily, Kent and I made some beautiful memories.

Kent and I had been furniture shopping and we bought an awesome new outdoor setting to take in our view and to catch the final few clear, gorgeous late-autumn days.

I was giving thanks for every moment we had with Kent before he left this morning for work again.

We had afternoon drinks on the new setting and then fed Lily her dinner there as the sun set. The box that it all came in was turned into a mini cubby for Lil by her daddy, and he jumped in and played with her.

The happiness that I felt was overwhelming yesterday. It would be lovely to be together every day without Kent having to work. I'll keep buying those lottery tickets!

Netball is evil

Wednesday night was my first netball practice. I thought I'd be fine since I'd been working out, and I was when it came to my cardio fitness. The other parts are where my wheels fell off. It seems that running, sprints, squats, lunges, burpies (don't ask – they should be outlawed), and then falling on your arse really doesn't do it for my body. I can't exactly move right now and when I do I look like my legs are made of stiff metal and I have a carrot up my butt. I am the walking/limping wounded.

I am so stiff that I need to use the sink in the ensuite to hang onto while I lower myself onto the loo.

I have killer grazing too – on both knees and one elbow but mostly on my PRIDE. I was running for a pass and touched the ball but it was getting away from me so I went that little bit too far and fell onto the asphalt court on my knees. Like coming in to land like a plane – *shreech, shreech, shreech!* There was blood, but I got up and kept playing – god forbid I looked like a sook.

After training we went to the pub for a drink and I made lots of jokes about my rustiness after three years of not playing. When I got home I bawled to Kent. I had expected so much more from myself.

Of course, hindsight is a wonderful thing, so I will point out the good and bad of the night.

THE BAD

I looked like a tool when I fell over; I can imagine the picture from behind (all bloody behind I'm sure!).

I was the slowest out of everyone when running or sprinting.

My legs felt like they were in concrete.

I had trouble catching and throwing well.

I could hardly run on the court when we finally got into game play, therefore my game play was shite!

THE GOOD

Three years ago when I last played I would not have been able to do half the running etc., but I managed to do it all this time.

I only walked about five paces in the court laps; the rest I jogged – very slowly – and was passed by everyone, but I did it.

I could get my breath back really quickly after all the running/sprints etc., it was just my legs that couldn't handle it.

I now realise I don't just want to be slim and fit, I want to be slim, FAST, and fit.

I know ways of making myself faster and I'm going to work on them as well as on Keith.

My knees will heal and my muscles will loosen (and in the meantime they are working off extra weight).

The only way is up. It can't get any worse, so it can only get better from now on.

I got into B1s.

So, here's what I give thanks for today: my lovely broken knees who worked damn hard for me, and I thank them for just coping with the flogging they got!

Still buggered

I wonder if I could be stiffer if a car ran me over? Not that I am asking for that at all! But I just wonder.

I would love a high Nanna bed, Nanna loo and Nanna chair right now.

Have seriously contemplated giving Lily to someone for a day or so while I recover as it is horrible trying to bend over, pick her up, kneel to bath her etc.

God, I need to keep looking after this body of mine to hopefully alleviate any early issues with getting around as I age.

Is that my lesson Universe? Don't stuff this body up because one day you'll be old and buggered?

Yeah, no doubt there is something more to it.

In the meantime, I will protest loudly and sulkily online as there is no one here to listen me besides two snoring puss-cats and one sleeping bub.

Nanna nap time? Mmmmmm…

Will lubricate my muscles with a few drinks at a 40th birthday party tonight – that should help!?

P.S. Here's what I'm thankful for today: my collar bone starting to appear again (sort of).

Ouch

Damn periods. I feel like Henny Penny – the sky is falling down today! Everything is wrong.

First, the scale said I have gained. What the…?!

Second, I'm in pain.

Third, the house is in a state.

Fourth, I haven't worked out in four days due to my knackered, post-training body.

Fifth, it is a public holiday and I have nothing planned as Lily and I are ALL ALONE. See? I am a bit melodramatic today.

I'm going to get out of my pjs, pop some Panadol, get moving, and tidy this house; put Lil to bed for a nap and workout on Keith, then we'll go to Ikea for some retail therapy.

Sympathy for little kids with skinned knees all over the world

My knees are still damn sore from my clutzy move at Netball practice last week. They are red, and the scabs are splitting, making my pants stick to them – youchy!

They might be infected. Oh well, I'm sure I won't die from scabby knees.

I do feel sorry for all those little kids out there in the world with sore, grazed knees – bless them!

On another note: the sky didn't fall down yesterday.

I did clean up the house and do a workout on Keith, and felt amazing. Then I went to Ikea with Lil and my mum and had a nice time. Mission accomplished for a day!

It's a bit of a *Groundhog Day* today because my house has been miraculously messed up again by my ever-exploring baby gal, and I am feeling a little glum.

I'm all decked out ready for a go on Keith, though. I bought Beyonce's album last week, which makes me MOVE! *All the single ladies… all the single ladies…* He he!

I have two more days to get two more workouts in before netball training Wednesday night. May my body be ready for another caning and may my arse fall off a bit more before so I don't look like a complete tool again! (As I'm typing this, I hear Leonie calling me 'Ms Perfect' and I laugh because that's just what I'm doing – self-sabotage is so ingrained huh?!)

One thing I am grateful for is two nights in a row of ten full hours of uninterrupted sleep – as in not one wee in the middle of the night for me, and not one peep from Miss Lily to disturb my gorgeous slumber. How lucky!

Could still go a few more hours right now. Mmm… lovely comfy, warm bed…

Blood Sugar Sex Magic

That's it – that's exactly what I am thankful for today – the Red Hot Chilli Peppers album 'Blood, Sugar, Sex, Magic'.

I have been rocking out to it today. Poor Lily has been subjected to her mum doing lots of crazy dance moves and singing every lyric to her with gusto!

Suck my Kiss!!!

Oh, yeah. Brings back great memories.

Funny how when 'Calificornication' came out I had no concept of California – it was so foreign and far away. Now I've been there and, well, the world doesn't seem such a big place like it did. I also feel so much more confident and self-assured. Isn't travel the most amazing form of liberation?!

Can't wait to do so much more travelling with my baby – Kent – and with our Miss Lily too.

Having a huge day of missing my man.

I am just lonely for him. Even if I was in a room of people I knew, I'd still be missing him. I miss my friend. xx

Only 10-ish more sleeps until we see him again. *sigh*

On a happier note, I have just tied a ribbon around Lily's baby doll and she is happily dragging it around the house, up chairs and over tables. Lucky she doesn't have a real brother or sister! Ha!

V is for...

Victory.

I had to buy a bra two sizes smaller across the back! My rocks in socks filled the F-cup though, so I am still busty, just not so chunky across the back. Woohoo!

Anyway, I give thanks for, well, my rack today.

It is still ok-looking in a bra.

So I pay homage to my knockers.

I have a horrible feeling...

... that my blog is boring you guys (sh)witless.

Maybe it's just my own stuff getting in the way here, but my mundane journaling may in fact be making you yaaaaaaawn. Hope not.

This may be coming from my 'I'm home alone with a 16-month-old child, and no job' thoughts. I'm not actually lonely for company as I have great friends and family around me, I think it is still a case of being lonely for Kent. He has the unfortunate job of listening to my daily ramblings, and when we only speak for about 20-30 minutes at the end of the day, I feel a little batty by then with all that I need to disclose – the good, the bad and the boring.

That's why this blog may be getting crappier by the minute – it is substituting my husband's ears.

I don't apologise for myself completely though, because as an extrovert I gather my energy from being with people. I told Kent last night that he better not leave me home alone too long because he may find me in the foetal position rocking in a corner when he gets back.

I think the head space I am committing to my weight-loss is also making me so 'into' myself and my thoughts/feelings that I am drowning in it.

I have been keeping busy with surface stuff at home, but my long-term plans and actions are just kinda floating along with the weight-loss wagon. That is what is in full control at the mo. See, if I was at work, I'd have something else to think about... woah... what am I THINKING! This is exactly where I want to be, just a bit more out of this maze of thoughts guiding me this way and that!

Am I sounding mad? Mmmm, thought so.

So, I guess if this is complete shite, you can, well... stop reading. So it is your choice my friends, but in the meantime I'll make no more apologies and keep belting out my little ditty posts (to stop myself rocking in the corner).

I give thanks for... yes, you guessed it – my computer and blog for linking me to the big, wide glorious online world!

Mwah, mwah! xxx

Cold but feeling content

Today is the coldest day we've had all autumn. It's wet, windy, and wonderful.

The rain is sparkling on the leaves in the afternoon light. The ground has had a good soak and our rain-water tanks have had a welcome top up.

Today's weather was not going to beat me from the beginning.

I rugged up in some warm clothes and headed out early with Lil for a quick shopping expedition.

Lily and I bought some sushi and I've now discovered we have two sushi monsters in the house. She can't get enough!

I guess I can give thanks for one of my favourite foods, and that I can still eat it post-Band! Mmmmmm!

Green is good!

Oh, wow! I made the BEST dish last night... if you could even call it that. My mum gave me a bunch of homegrown spinach and I cooked an onion and a leek in a bit of organic coconut butter and then added a heap of chopped spinach. The delicate smell of coconut was amazing, and when I tasted it, well... it knocked my socks off! It was *sooooo* good. I just added a couple of cashew nuts and a wee bit of sea salt, and away I went. It was even better than my sushi – I KID YOU NOT!!

Well must fly as I am picking up my first subscription fruit and veg box today from local organic Adelaide Hills growers.

Can't wait to see what goodies I have to cook with over the next week!

P.S. This is purely for my husband's info but I have a terrible craving for getting silly drunk and making love all night – hurry up home! Te he!!!

Taking stock

I've had a few lightbulb moments in the past two days.

I had an awesome Saturday night after netball (we won by 12 goals!) at the club rooms where I caught up with locals I hadn't seen for six months or more. There were many comments re how good and healthy I looked, and that made me really happy. I am feeling a little cautious in being too cocky about how I feel in myself at the moment, because it could very easily change. I don't think I will stop losing weight the way I am going, but if I fell pregnant or say injured myself it could put a halt to it for a while (maybe I'd even gain some back?).

One blog I read mentioned that weight-loss is a constant fight even when you hit your goal weight. I get that, but I don't care to see it as a 'fight' as such, more of an awareness and being conscious of your body and your emotions. I don't want to 'fight' with anyone, especially myself!!

Anyway, all I am saying is that I am calling it, Universe. I can see that I could stumble here and there, but I'm prepared to keep going forever. I am really enjoying my newfound leanness, but I also understand it is just my exterior. I am made of strong stuff emotionally and spiritually and I am committed to evolving.

Thanks for putting it into perspective for me anyway. I appreciate your messages and I am trying to listen to all of them.

So, onto what I give thanks for besides my physical self:

My darling girl for making me a mother – thanks for choosing me...

I did have my closest call with some food getting stuck in my Band yesterday whilst we were out. I bolted down some chicken salad and then I went quiet. Kent asked what he'd done wrong. He honestly thought he'd done something to upset me. No, I was just hoping the food wouldn't fly right back out of my mouth if I opened it! I went to the toilet, but was so scared someone would hear me that I found the disabled one instead. By the time I got there the pain stopped as the food passed through the band. Phew!!! Anyway, lesson learned for now. Eat slowly and CHEW, dammit!

Damn mother's guilt

I have been contemplating what my life would be like if Lily had one more day in childcare during the week.

Since Kent has been away I can really feel my stress levels rising. I can't ask my folks to have Lily without plenty of notice and to pencil it into their diaries – if I do, it has to be for a damn good reason, not just that I am losing it being alone with her. *eye roll

I don't know if she is any harder these days; maybe more demanding of my attention, yes, but maybe it's just that it is solely up to *me* to care for her??

Anyway, I have now been offered one more day at childcare, and of course I am already feeling GUILTY!!

Why should I put her in childcare when I am not working? Can't I cope with just one child?

What about all the working mums with two or more kids?? What about the cost? What will my parents and friends think? Yada yada.

Gee, we are *soooo* good at guilt, aren't we?!

Take a look at me flaying myself. Whip it, whip it good!

I think it's smart for me to take this extra day because I have been questioning my mental health recently and it's not faring too well. Lily adores being at childcare and she will love the extra day. Kent's work away is supposed to be finished around June/July, but who knows what he'll take on then – or if it will really be finished. My folks go away in July for six weeks, so that is when I am literally alone if Kent is still working away.

Yes, two days childcare a week is going to be good for me.

I didn't ever sign up to be a single mum for the majority of the time. I assumed my married life would be shared with my husband and that he would be there to share in the life of his children. But you know what they say: assumption is the mother of all fuck-ups.

Oh, well, tomorrow is another day and I'm sure the Universe intended to put this in our path for a reason. I'll ponder that now... bugger the guilt!

Kicking it

Keith the Killer cross trainer kicked my arse today. Or, should I say, I kicked HIS arse – beating my best distance by heaps!

Keith + Beyonce = Killer Goddess Workouts. Beyonce makes me rock while I bust my butt on Keith up and down his imaginary hills!

I am crammed into our ever-filling shed amongst massive guillotine machines and cars but it's ok; I will take Keith wherever he is! Te he!

Keith clears my mind and makes me feel good even when my baby has gone away again for work. Oh well, two more weeks solo to work on my fitness.

This morning I have had to be within arms' reach of Miss Lil as she is missing her daddy already. I decided to watch a couple of TV programs I recorded, and Ned – one of our puss-uns – smooched in to get some cuddles. Well, Lily wanted him bad for her own headlock/cuddles, so he was subjected to tough but overjoyed Lily-love all morning.

He remained purring the whole time he was laid on and dragged around. So I give thanks for my patient puss, Ned, today. Bruce, the other cat, was clever and stayed up on his pole out of her reach..

Blue

Just a bit sad today. A lonely Friday. Yes, baby, I am ready for you to come home early. The change of shift to 10 days on 4 days off, is just what we need. More time together. xx

Lily has been a doll; think I might nab her when she's in a deep sleep and put her into bed with me tonight. Bubba & mumma cuddles.

Choccy then warm bed very soon.

Tomorrow will be better, I'm sure.

Wins make me happy

I had an absolute ball playing netball yesterday! We beat the top team (last year's premiers) and we weren't expecting to get close to them. The opposition team was filled with players I have played against for decades – lots of experience and skill. The game was friendly, and I thought the contest was of a really high standard. Love those types of games. Often younger teams can get a bit stroppy (I remember being bitchy myself), but us 'oldies' are out to have fun and enjoy the contest.

Anyway, it picked up my day and completely turned things around from miserable to happy. I felt that I played well, too, and I'm starting to feel a little quicker on the court.

The morning was filled with cooking more of my organic produce. I made beetroot and choccy brownies, which are lovely, and an apple crumble that is now in the freezer waiting for Kent to come home.

Oh!! A funny thing happened yesterday:

Keith is becoming famous. Someone was apparently chatting about me and said I was lucky to have a personal trainer.

"You're not talking about Keith, are you?"

"Yes, that's his name!"

Well the girl in the know fell about laughing and told the other girl that Keith was my cross trainer not my personal trainer. "He's just a machine!" she laughed.

How funny is that?! I just assumed that I'd explained Keith to everyone by now, but obviously not. Think that story is going to stick around forever! lol

Ailsa in her netball uniform

Head or body hunger?

I've been hungry for the past few days... and I have been eating!

Friday, I knew it was emotional because I was so blue and lonely. I knew I was trying to stuff down the feelings with anything I could lay my hands on. Whatever I ate wasn't 'filling the void'.

The last two days I've still been focussed on food, so maybe I'm premenstrual.

Today, I'm just going with it and eating as much as I want earlier in the day and trying to have less in the pm (for good digestion). We'll see how I go. Two crumpets with cheese, a tea, and a coffee down and I'm starting to feel... well, full!

Keith will help once I get my gal into bed for her nap. Keith always takes away my appetite for a while.

Oh, and Lil has a bit of a cold and a horrid cough, so I'm going to take her to the doctor later. She ended up in bed with me last night, which meant my sleep was very broken. There you go – being tired always makes me hungrier too...

It all makes sense now.

The 'Queen' (Kent) arrives home Friday, which means more snackies over the weekend.

See? I am stuck in my head again; not trusting the process or my body.

Listen Ailsa, listen...

Positive change

It's amazing how easy it is to get caught up in what the number on the damn scale is saying rather than taking stock of all the positive behavioural changes I'm experiencing – pretty much on a daily basis!

Last night I got back to basics and started repeating my affirmation: *I love and approve of myself exactly as I am.* I asked for some help from the Universe, some guide to get me away from my negative thoughts, and that is what came to me – love yourself and trust that all is well in my world

Queeny

The Queen is home! Te he.

Lily is so excited to spend time with her daddy.

I've done the usual – cooked up a storm for him, bought special snackies and presents for him, and basically got ready for hanging out and just 'living the dream' while he's home. Chats, drinks, cuddles, experiences instead of usual 'work' around the house/Lily/routines etc.

Wish we could it for longer.

Soon, I'm sure.

Two lines = life has changed

I've made myself a strong cup of tea. I need it.

Just peed on a stick and it came up with two lines. Yes, two. Which means… um yes, I am pregnant! *gasp*

I am waiting for Kent to get back from the workshop and I am bursting to tell him, but I want to show him the stick and see his expression. I had to start to write what I'm feeling because otherwise my thoughts might lift me off my feet and float me off on the winds, it feels so surreal.

I first saw one line appear and thought, oh thank goodness,- just one – false alarm… then the second one appeared before my eyes, glowing with anticipation of my reaction, I'm sure.

Straight into the shower where I doused myself with warm water as my heart soared and my tummy filled with excited and scared butterflies! What is Kent going to think? He's going to be completely stressed out, I'm sure. Poor bloke.

The last time he was back I couldn't get enough of him. I had a tell-tale sign of ovulation on Wednesday (the day before he got home), so I thought we had missed the ovulation boat (but I wasn't convinced).

I started taking the pill prior to my Lap Band op because I was afraid that I might fall pregnant. I decided to stop taking the pill once I'd lost a considerable amount of weight, because it didn't seem right to stop nature if it was meant to be. We had to do IVF to get Lily, surely, it was a long shot falling pregnant naturally? On the other hand, I felt deep in my goddess womb that indeed it was possible, and if it did happen we were truly supposed to have a second child.

Now, I'm in tears of gratitude. Droplets of amazement and joy are splashing the keys. What a gorgeous miracle.

I thought I could be pregnant as I was two days past my period due date. Even though it's only been two months since I stopped the pill, my cycle was generally spot on.

So it seems not only did I ovulate with style, but Kent's supposedly dodgy sperm (wrapped in antibodies due to his past surgery), have pushed through and done their job! I am stunned with how amazing it is!

Of course, as each thought enters my mind, I am thinking this pregnancy may not last; I may miscarry. Or I could have something wrong detected in-utero and might have to choose to terminate or not. Termination... maybe that is what Kent would want even now. Surely not? Maybe... We were always going to be happy enough with just one child, weren't we?

Oh, you see how important it is for me to get all of this down before I blow up my brain with my thoughts?!

Anyway, Lily was waiting for me when I got out of the shower. I showed her my tummy and she patted it and kissed it as if she knew that a potential brother or sister is residing inside – so divine. A moment I'll always remember. She's going to love being an older sister. She loves her bubba doll and helping with the baby and 'chores' – feeding the baby, wiping its face etc.

Oh gosh, what about my mum and dad? They are going to be shocked, and probably both incredibly happy and frightened of the burden of two grandchildren. My mother-in-law is going to be thrilled... so is my sister-in-law, and aunt and Nanna... Gosh, everyone is going to be excited.

I think I want to keep this one a secret for a while though, just in case we don't make it to 12 weeks.

I have already felt a bit of morning sickness (ms). Yesterday I felt hungover without being hungover... just like with Lil, but that was from week 5 to 15 – horrid 24-hr nausea without vomiting. Can I do this without Kent being home? Yes. I am tough. Oh my god... two kids! Bigger car. Need to sort out another bedroom... guests will sleep where? Lounge room?

If this is really it, then it's good timing. The Universe got me when I was a bit keen. My life hasn't returned to pre-baby yet. I can go the slog of the first year with a baby again without it feeling too distant. Lily and bubs (typing that made me crack a huge smile) will be just over two years apart. Maybe another girl? That would be divine. But a bubba boy? Kent would be ecstatic. Yes, I will want to know at 20 weeks what it is, but not tell anyone. Oh! Excited, thrilled, scared witless! Names? Birthing options?

My weight-loss and boob lift put off for a little while? That's ok, we'll get there. I can still see me losing weight during the pregnancy. Keith will still be great for me and bubs.

Travel? Well, that's going to be on hold for a while. The Darwin holiday won't be so flash without a bunch of beers, but that's ok too. I'll be feeling good for Lily in the morning. Overseas travel was probably not going to be until next year at least. Kent can still go away for work, but we'll need to reassess in the future. Work? Well, thank goodness I haven't gone back to anything yet. I knew I was holding that space for something else.

Oh god, it's only 3pm. I think Kent's going to be hours yet. I am going to bust with this info.

The pregnancy test is sitting in the en suite. I keep going in to check it. I was always told that pregnancy tests never give false positives – false negatives, but not false positives. It came up quickly too, not like Lily's tests, which were faint and scratchy. Twins? Triplets? Sheeze, why scare myself? Stop, mind, stop.

Let it go. It is absolutely meant to be...

I feel sick. Maybe the tea? lol

Everyone's reactions

So I waited for over five hours yesterday for Kent to get home so I could tell him the news face to face. The poor boy was shattered from a heavy day of labour at the workshop and I then hit him with it. I gave Lily the pee test to give him (she did, then whined that she wanted it back – bit of a tricky moment).

He tried to read it without his glasses, upside down and didn't get it until I said I was probably pregnant. Well, he smiled, but defeat loomed in his eyes. "I thought we were only going to have one child," he said, still smiling, but his lips were getting heavier. I was prepared for it, but it also took my breath away. I felt that I had done something wrong; that I had wrecked our lives. He said he'd need a while to process it, but he was still kind and loving with me and Lily. I just felt despair.

All night I contemplated termination but knew I couldn't do it. I was trapped between a rock and a hard place. The rock would be if I had the baby then our lives as we know it now (and the light at the end of the tunnel) would be gone for at least another two to three years. My weight-loss will cease, I may even gain it all back, and any freedom to just be me will be gone for years. The hard place was that if I chose to terminate I would be cheating myself because deep down I now know I want to become a mother of two.

I woke to Kent leaving for work. Another two weeks until he is home. He held me and said that everything would be all right. That it would be fun to have another bubba running around the house. He said he felt the same shock and fear when we found out we were pregnant with Lily, and that worked out in the end. He made me feel so much better. He said termination wasn't what we want. He loves us. I'm so glad.

No breakfast, and then a trip to the doctor to confirm that I am indeed pregnant.

I quickly rang Kent to confirm the test and asked if I can tell my folks, and asked him to tell his. I then rushed over to my parents as my mum was about to leave for Pilates, and told both Mum and Dad together. They were excited, shocked... but overall happy and positive for me. I wasn't expecting such a warm response. I still felt like I'd done something wrong. We were all happy with just Lily. Anyway, I'm relieved by their reaction because they will be the closest to me besides Kent, and I need them on my side. My father saw that I was in two minds and said I should try and find the joy in this pregnancy, like the last one, as it is important to be joyful, not sad. That was lovely... and I will.

I am lost in a day of thick fog. Everything is heavy with the knowledge of this pregnancy. I feel like the Universe is cloaking me in mist, so I can snuggle up and process this in my own time, in my own sacred place.

I know what to do. I know to let the worries flow off me and to rejoice in the wonder of the miracle. I know to find joy in each moment as it is meant to be.

So, the process begins again – the sacred time of growing another baby inside me. I need to get some folate and another gorgeous journal, so I can write to this fluttering little soul in my womb.

Years ago, before falling pregnant, I sat looking across our valley and visualised Lily coming to me as a white light and entering my womb and then the other week I sat in the same spot and thought about another child coming and choosing me as their mother... just as I did, a butterfly floated straight to me. It felt like a sign that another baby was on its way. Another sign was a ladybug sitting on Lily's hair the other day. I saw it as a lucky, gorgeous sign of something good. It was beautiful. I let it go outside after showing an amazed Lily.

Goddess, womanly knowledge, and instinct is wondrous.

Blessings and welcome to my second child. xx

Still knocked up

So I did my third pregnancy test yesterday just to check that in fact I was still pregnant. I'm still in disbelief... and yep, I'm still pregnant.

I found a teeny tiny autumn leaf with flashes of red and gold through it – it felt like a little sign from the autumn-conceived bubba. I've kept it and put it in his or her journal.

I've managed to keep the news quiet. It's sort of good to keep it a little secret because I am fearful I'll miscarry. I dreamt of doing so last night; vivid blood clots, and there was nothing I could do. It was horrible.

I have a bung neck; strained it sneezing the other day – what the...?! I know neck issues are usually because you are fighting change. Funny that Kent had one too. We just have to go with the process and trust that all is well in our world.

I'm a little more tired than usual, though of course sleep has been messed up with all my thoughts, dreams, aches and pains over the last few nights.

I felt a bit of nausea this morning and all I want to eat is hot, comfort food – cheese, bread, pastry and sweet drinks, chai lattes etc. I can still give pickles and mustard a good nudge, too.

Other possible pregnancy symptoms are a fuzzy brain and tender breasts.

I hold up my top each morning and tell Lily the baby is in my tummy, and she kisses my tummy (think she thinks it's an ouch because my Band op scars are there). It's cute anyway.

Just went to a morning tea with a heap of kiddies running around. A few babies too, and I felt ok (and a little excited) about having another one. Lily loved looking at the babies, which was a great sign. I think I'm going to do ok this time. I feel more confident and relaxed.

The scales were up this morning – boo!

Hope that I can still lose some more weight with this pregnancy.

I had a go on Keith yesterday and felt fine of course. Today I might just have a nap rather than workout. Then I'll have another chai latte this afternoon, and maybe some cheese and gerkins on biscuits...

Mmm, maybe I'll have some now...

Feeling precious

I'm feeling a bit nervous about playing Netball today. I just don't know if I'll have the energy or drive to play well. I'm afraid of being pregnant on the court. I'm sure it will be fine...but this morning I just want to stay in the warm with cheese toasties

My neck is pretty good, but a Netball game may flare it up again.

I'm just feeling a bit precious – my hormones are probably kicking in... everything is a bit too hard. I just want to be rescued – someone please come and clean my house, care for Lily and make me food while I sit on the lounge or nap in bed – thanks! Doing it alone, while Kent works away may be a little harder than I first anticipated.

I bought a pregnancy magazine yesterday which is making my brain pop as I look at all the big bellies and stories about birthing – might have to put it away for a few more weeks till I'm ready. My Goddess is saying to free my mind a little by getting the house straight and then enjoy the time I get to spend with family and friends today. That's my aim anyway.

I have a super cute waistcoat that I'm going to wear over a tank top and jeans tonight...may as well wear it while I can before I pop out!

Word's out

Netball was ok. Got a little puffed for a while but not sure if that was my fitness or bubs. We won by just one goal when we were up by 15 at one stage – eek! Shocking mental state of our team; we got all frazzled and they capitalised on it. Boo!

Anyway, I went out to the netball dinner last night as planned. I wore my cute waist coat, which lots of the girls said looked nice.

I quietly sipped on soda and lime drinks and chatted away, then thought that it would be a perfect time to tell all my local girlfriends at once (I'm so shite at keeping secrets!). So I started, and then my darling friend Trace made a lovely announcement to the room of Summertown netball girls about me being pregnant and they all promptly erupted into applause and wolf whistles.

I got tons of hugs and kisses from everyone. It was a moment I'll remember forever. I felt the love all right!

Jealousy is a curse

I had an overwhelmingly horrible feeling this morning – jealousy. I was speaking with a friend and she told me about her great party night on Saturday, and how there's another one on this Saturday… then she said she's going to netball training and the gym as I've inspired her.

"Look where it's got me now- knocked up!" I said with a sarcastic smile.

I drove off and felt awful. Why? Because I am jealous that she is living my life – MY life that I had just 10 days ago before I found out I was pregnant. I was the one who was getting fit, getting ready for the parties and getting my own life back. Now I am back at what feels like square one.

I know it isn't all that bad; I will be at that point again soon – it will come again fast, I'm sure.

It was just such an overwhelming emotion that I had to nail it down and call it what it was.

I'm going to jump on Keith now for a positive perspective.

Will get back to you with a more happier post in an hour or two!

Things have evened out

So my theory worked yesterday – Keith made my world better.

It's ok to be jealous at times, as long as you know what you are feeling and understand that it's a choice to sit in it or move on.

I chose to move on.

I had a great run at training last night, too. Felt a bit more nervous about falling when I was running in some of our drills, but apart from that, I felt fit and well.

I am really keen to keep up my fitness level throughout this pregnancy.

Haven't caught you up on my brief Roxby Downs trip. It was very quiet as Kent had to work, but it gave me space to sit, rest, and THINK in my hotel room. Roxby itself is simply… pink, from the red earth it sits on. From the plane it looked like a swirling pink landscape with black spots – gorgeous. I had dinner just with Kent one night, which was a real treat. He's been a bit damn cute thinking of boy's names (we have a girl's name chosen). I love that he seems more 'into' this pregnancy. It's so nice to share it with him. It was great to fly up and see him as it gives me a better perspective of where he's been working. It's always been good when he's flown me to places where he's working.

Think it could be a key to me feeling relaxed about the work away if I'm somehow included. It always makes me so proud to see Kent working, because he's amazing. Yes, maybe I'm a bit biased but it's the truth!

Anyway, the flight up and back was short and sweet. I had a moment where I was given bickies and cheese and a cup of tea, and I was in heaven – no little arm grabbing at me. Sitting above the clouds in the glorious sun, it was divine!

Coming home to my gorgeous gal was divine too. She'd had a ball with her Nanna and Puppa… but was ready for Mummy loves.

Ciao for now. x

Clouded head

My head is foggy; clouded by nausea. Yes, I think morning (all day) sickness is kicking in, and I am starting to pop out already too!! What the...? Maybe it's because I have been over-scrutinizing my body changes and now they are going backwards... or outwards! Anyway, I panicked last night thinking it must be twins or more... or maybe no baby, just a blighted ovum or something? Oh, how I mess with my own head. It could have also been the massive amount of pizza I ate last night.

Must away and lie down. Hoping that being home with m/s rather than at work will be better. At least I don't have to face anyone if I don't want to.

Bye. xx

Officially hibernating

That's it.

I am not leaving the lounge/bed for the next two months unless necessary and unless I feel well enough.

Lucky Lily likes breakfast cereal because that's about all I can eat happily at the moment. She and I have been sharing. Actually, she's been hogging the spoon whenever bowls of the stuff come out. She and I are still in our PJs at 5.30pm – the house looks like a bomb has gone off but I don't care.

I figure that if I really feel like something normal to eat, like stir-fried veggies, I will go out and buy it. Couldn't begin to make my own. Nausea is stopping me in my tracks when trying to make meals for Lil – even scrambled eggs – blurgh! Iced cold water with brown lime cordial takes the edge off.

Oh, Kent, hurry up and get home before Lily gets scurvy!

I have been giving her oranges and avocado (no cooking involved) and yoghurt, so she's getting some good stuff.

This bubba is giving me the same grief as Lil – I could only eat cereal and drink brown lime cordial for weeks in my early pregnancy with her. At least I know that it does end, and at least I'm not at work. Getting outside in the fresh air makes me feel good too.

I was thinking that it will be nice to spend the next nine months with Lily before the baby is born – it will be our special time together. She's trying to send a fax, presumably, at the moment – fiddling with all the buttons on the machine and grinning at me. *cute*

Can't wait for a little down time in Darwin in the sun. Can't wait to see Lil and her daddy together again; they'll be besotted for days!

Bath time for us. Off to splash around with the girl. xx

Where do I belong in blogland?

I don't feel like I fit into Lap Band blog land anymore. Everyone is losing weight and gaining their lives back and I'm well, still losing weight but gaining a more complicated life.

Maybe I need to check out some Mother Goddess blogs.

Maybe I need to start a new blog of my own where I fit perfectly. Today has obviously been a bit better nausea-wise for me to think of anything except food. I seem to be consumed with thoughts of what I can eat but then everything makes me feel sick.

Today I had nausea-free moments – only moments, but they gave me a bit of a break. I am taking Vit B and ginger root tabs; hope that's what is doing it and they keep helping!

Be interesting to speak to my Band GP to see what she'll advise. Maybe she'll have some good stats about patients getting back on track and losing all their excess weight post-baby? That's what I'm after – some inspiration.

My boy gets home tomorrow – can't WAIT! We've all missed each other; he us, and us him.

Then we get to kick back on our family holiday in Darwin! Wahoo!

Happy days! xx

P.S. Today I'm grateful for:

Lily doing pile-ons on Ned the cat – he was purring the entire time. She kept pushing him on his side and lying on top of him. She did it about 10x and he was still purring. He loves her!!

Just put me down now – please

Ok, so get ready for a purge post. Apologies, but it has to be said.

My life right now is SHITTY.

Pregnancy can be a cruel, cruel thing. This one is hurting me a lot already. I am nauseated all day – it is just wearing me down.

I have a sinus infection... or maybe it's simply stuffy head like I had with Lil? I can't taste anything, but I get phantom tastes in my mouth that freak me out. The other day I had the taste of soap or shampoo in my mouth like I'd accidentally got some in my mouth in the shower. Farking horrible.

My digestion is wrong too; either all blocked up or the opposite.

I have raging desires for certain types of food and then they disperse immediately, often before I get to eat them.

The only thing that is working in me is my TEMPER. Fuck this Universe. I am not pleased with feeling so crap!!!!

I have obviously been a JOY to be around. Particularly stuck on a holiday in Darwin (just ask Kent).

I tried, I honestly did try to be as positive and happy and as WELL as possible on the trip, but I had a few mini-meltdowns when Kent did dumb-arse things (yes, baby, face it – they were). Generally, I am better at reining in my previous controlling behaviour, but right now it has to be my fucking way or nothing!!

Kent is fighting it tooth and nail, but he won't win of course. He may as well let me rant and ignore me (but not the essential bits about doing laundry and the dishes etc., lol).

I know that this too shall pass. Once the nausea is gone in possibly another eight weeks or less (please less, please, please) I will be able to focus on being positive again. Right now, there is no use. I need a bullet – shoot me, put me down... put me out of my misery.

I have lost more weight, but I'd give anything to be the size of two houses again if it meant I wouldn't feel sick!

I'm going to the doctor tomorrow re my nose and to ask for help with the nausea. If she says try dry crackers and ginger I will throttle her. Give me the good stuff, NOTHING ELSE WORKS! Arrrghhhhhhhhhhhhh!!

I'm not feeling oh so positive about what this baby will mean for our lives either. I mean seriously, we are locked in now. I won't be surprised if Kent pleads with anyone to give him his next fly-away job tomorrow so he can leave my sorry arse and the pressure of family life. If I could, I'd do the fucking same!

All I ask right now is for the house to be clean (it makes me feel sicker when it's not), Lily to be fed decent meals, and plenty of time for me to lie down because that's the only thing that can ease the nausea.

And some nice stuff

Just a quickie so Kent can see that I'm not just bitching about him and the world. A few things I figured out on the holiday in Darwin:

1. There is nothing more attractive than a father who is genuinely enjoying spending time with his child/children. Kent was so attentive to Lily – she was his shadow for the whole trip. They both adored each other's company.
2. Sun, salt air, and fresh tropical fruit can ease some complaints (for a while).
3. Why the hell don't we all get up to the tropics in winter? It is bliss!
4. 30+ sunscreen and hats can still provide you with enough protection to not burn, but enjoy a wee bit of holiday tan.
5. Justified complaints to hotel management can get you an upgrade – or two, in our case. We ended up in a one-bedroom apartment... awesome.
6. Don't settle for a hotel room, get an apartment with kiddies in tow (if you can afford it).
7. Life changes when you have kids. You look for the nearest supermarket for milk and nappies rather than the nearest bottle shop for beer and champagne.

How to wish time away

It seems that next week I'll be in my 10th week of pregnancy – how's that for wishing time away (yes, I've been wishing this first trimester away since the nausea hit). 10 weeks is a quarter of the way through this pregnancy. Wahoo! Love it!

Living life through packets of different dry biscuits and whatever does it for me that minute, lying down as much as possible and going to bed by 8pm is making my days fly.

I have realised I am a bit off chocolate and coffee. Normally they are my daily joys. I am today into lemon – sweet lemon pudding that is. Mmmm.

Cups of tea can settle the tum. Exercise is still amazing. At netball training I felt 100% while I was on the court.

I had an appointment with my specialist GP at the Lap Band clinic and she was very happy for us – excited actually, which was cute. She said that being pregnant with the Band is fine as long as I am not vomiting, and the baby is growing as it should. If either changes I can have all the fluid in my Band removed. The GP also said now is the time to concentrate on the baby and myself, not the Band and losing weight. Good stuff. Can't concentrate on anything but feeling sick right now anyway.

By the way, Kent is being an absolute doll! I've told him he has been so helpful and doing wonderful things like thinking ahead for Lily and I and our needs, that he is being like a wife to me – the biggest compliment he could ever get. **Every woman needs a wife**.

He's been home with us for over two weeks now, and may still be around for another week. His parents are coming to stay next week, which will be nice. My mother-in-law helps me so much, thank goodness. They'll be excited to see the changes in Lil. She's such a cracker at 18 months old – her personality is getting cheekier and brighter every day. Her vocab is increasing, as is her awareness of what she *doesn't* want to do. She's great at tanties until I get her to laugh it off with me. No point getting cranky – it is her right to set her own boundaries at times. Let me remember this as the tantrums increase!

Anyhoo, 8.14pm – past my bedtime. Horizontal eases the sicky tum.

I'm off to bed.

Night, night. xx

Bump

Not sure how long I can play netball before I look visibly pregnant. Today I've put on my uniform and feel a bit thicker in the waist. It looks like chub, which is good... even though I had got the chub on my tum down to almost flat. Boo! We have an issue with players over the next few weeks; we'll be down to six players (three short) when I am 11 and 12 weeks. I'll be needed, and I want to play. After that I think I may call it a day. I'm feeling more aware of my pregnant body, getting a bit slower on the court and I'll be showing more. Ah, I'll see how it goes – week by week – and if I can't play then I won't. Everyone will understand.

The best thing about netball is that I get out in the fresh air and see all the gals; keep up with what's going on and don't stay a complete hermit. It is also MY time – not as a mummy or a wife, but as ME. I can still go out and watch the games, I suppose, if I can't play. Compromises, compromises!

One strong little heartbeat!

Phew!! Just one strong little heartbeat at my first scan today. The OB played a trick and said there were two sacs, but then said, "but just one baby – the other sac is your bladder!"

I called him a bastard. Kent's face was priceless for a split second; mine was probably the same: pure terror! Then we all laughed.

Anyway, so far, so good. The baby is about 9½ weeks – same as my calculations and we have another more comprehensive scan at 12 weeks (well, it will be 13 and one day).

He/she moved around delicately and almost gave me a little wave and thumbs up. Very cute. Made my heart melt.

So, my first wish for the baby was to be just *one* baby not two or more. Thanks for granting my wish, Universe! I have a few more to ask of you, too, so please listen out for my quiet, hopeful requests. xx

Back to waiting for this nausea to pass, then I'm going to throw a party for myself!! Celebrate living instead of just existing.

Kent has been excited by his future in the new Adelaide office that will be opening soon. He may be based more in Adelaide than FIFO work. All in all, positive and exciting for him and us.

Today I'm starting to think about getting my life back again once I have this baby.

Anyway, I now need a little couch time. I am busy cooking up a baby!

Blessings. xxx

Lily's bathtime

Blessings

I'm feeling happy and blessed leading up to my birthday tomorrow. Always a nice time on your birthday to reflect how lucky you are. Well, that's my aim anyway. Years ago, I used to moan about my birthday and Christmas being crappy, now I know it's up to me to change things, not anyone else!

Tomorrow, Kent and I are dropping Lil off to childcare and then getting some lunch. Should be nice and relaxing. I am looking forward to cake, too. Come to think of it, last night I woke dreaming about a creamy, custardy, iced cake... mmm. Funny pregnancy dreams!

I just got off Keith for the first time in a month! It was fantastic! Can feel my legs and bum and tum. Bubs felt fine, and the cardio exercise has eased the m/s for a moment. Actually, my m/s seems to be pretty good in the mornings if I eat breakfast and go slow. The afternoons/evenings are a write-off, but maybe, just maybe, things are turning around??!!

I've had several texts, calls, and emails from friends asking if I want to do something for my birthday in case Kent was away and I was alone. I'm touched they thought of me! Blessings abound! Friends are wonderful things! xx

I've been spoilt with Kent being home; he's still the best 'wife' a girl can have – cooking, changing pooey nappies, bathing, feeding, cleaning up and after Lily etc., plus, he's working hard to fix our rain-water system – a huge job!

He's back to work on Monday. Not sure of the future roster; hope it's kind to us. Gosh I am going to miss him *sooo* much! Apart from being helpful around the place, his company and friendship has been what's got me through the last few weeks. He and Lil are the lights in my life.

We had a look at a video recording of Lily one year ago and she wasn't even crawling, just lying down with her head up grinning at the puss-cat and me. It shows how quickly things change when that only felt like a minute ago. Gives us both hope this new bubba will be as cute and mobile as Lily is now. We are really enjoying her and all the cute things she does at 18 months old.

Must away and eat before I get really ill again.

Will be noting all my blessings today and tomorrow.

It's a big list! xx

B'day blessings – 7/7

B'day blessings (so far at 9.16am):

Waking up to a warm cosy house with Kent and Lily still fast asleep while the fog and mist surrounds our home on the hill.

The happy anticipation of hearing from people today and spending time with family.

My baby girl saying "hello" to me when I opened the bedroom door and coming to give me a big cuddle.

Getting a funny card from Kent and Lily (with her drawing in it). She was so excited to see it get opened.

Watching Lily holding her daddy's hand and smiling as she walked up the driveway to the shed – little chubby bubba legs!

Five minutes to myself to blog, have a coffee, and chill while Kent drops Lil off to childcare then off to have a hot shower and get dressed for my day out – yay! xx

3pm and cheese

It seems 3pm is when my wheels fall off the nausea train, before then it's not too bad really. It also seems that today, cheese is doing it for me, i.e. a cheeseburger and a cheese toastie. God help me if this baby is going to end up one of those people that only eats white or pale-yellow things.

I can hear Miss Lily saying "Mumma, Mumma" in the other room – too cute. So many new words coming out of her mouth every day. This morning was bottle and sticks (for the fire).

My parents have headed overseas for six weeks today. I am on cats, house, garden, mail, grandparents' duty. I am planning to do a good, gracious job and not let myself get stressed out. Lily and I will potter through the next few weeks alone (when Kent is away working) and enjoy the simple things in life like afternoon sleeps and maybe sleeps with me in the big bed on occasions too. Mmm bubba cuddles.

I am planning on pissing this morning sickness off soon too (hear that, Universe!), then I'll probably be ravenous. But at least I will get to really enjoy a meal again.

I'll be 11 weeks on Sunday, then I'll be in my 12th week next week.

Settle down raging hormones, please!

Dreams

Wow, forgot how intense pregnancy dreams can be. From dreams of house fires and dying, to dreams about cream cakes, and my favourite last night – being bedded by three men, one of them Kent and two other magical men who were mythical creatures and right into my complete pleasure. What more could a girl want?! Ba ha ha!

Now, where to find these gorgeous mythical men in real life??? I'm sure Kent wouldn't mind me meeting them (not!).

Today is a doozie, stormy day. Trees down everywhere and roads closed all around us.

Managed to get to my folks' house and get the puss-cats sorted. Now to staying dry and warm inside and getting Miss Lily to sleep rather than playing in her cot – cheeky gal.

I'm ill again. Off to make a cheese toastie....

My new coat

Baby it's cold outside...

Yes, it's cold outside and my baby has left me home alone again.

Kent has flown out for 10 days work today.

Lily and I are on our lonesome...

Because I was feeling a bit down, I stopped into a Laura Ashley shop. Now normally I could say I am not a Laura Ashley kinda gal; I've never bought anything from the shop, which is a tad pricey and well... floral.

But today when I stopped, I saw a gorgeous coat for 70% off it's normal crazy price. It was a smaller size, so I thought, *no chance of fitting into it, but I'll give it a whirl.* Well, lo and behold, it fitted! And so did a black woollen top and a black and grey skirt. All of which were on sale!

And baby, it won't be so cold outside without you in my new snuggly coat which, by the way, says the colour is pudding. NO pudding here! Just goddess curves, thank you very much!!

Ahh, the joys of good retail therapy! xx

Six months

It's Happy Six Months for me today!

I had my op on January 13, 2010, and have lost many kilos since then. Amazing.

Still a bit disappointed that my momentum was halted due to my pregnancy, but maybe there is another side to it.

I've been thinking that it takes a while to get used to your shrinking size when you lose a lot of weight. Lots of people notice and sometimes their comments and questions are almost intrusive and hurtful, because you don't feel any different inside. I am still that same person, so sometimes the compliments about my smaller size make me feel like I wasn't good enough for them at my larger size.

By sitting at my present weight throughout my pregnancy – give or take a few kilos – I have much more time to settle myself emotionally into this weight (and other people will get used to it too!). I am already feeling more like 'me'. I feel like those larger days are behind me and I can only go down from here; though if this was it for the weight-loss, I think I'd still be very happy.

I do have unfinished business though, and once I have the baby and settle into having two beautiful children, I will again be able to focus on ME.

So I'm sort of taking a well-deserved break to cook up this little one and then feel renewed and ready again. The sometimes-destructive mental state I can get in when I watch the scales can piss off for a while too. Which can only be good!

Am I learning, Universe? Surrender and trust the process? All is well in my world and divine timing is always occurring? Yes, I think so. It feels right.

12 weeks today

Today I am 12 weeks into my pregnancy. I have a scan tomorrow and then once those results come back and they are a.o.k, I'll be able to rest more easily.

I am only going to play one more game of netball as I'm starting to feel my uterus pop out. It is hard, and making me feel slower on my feet. Next Saturday will be my last time on the court. I just didn't feel up to scratch when I played yesterday, and I was penalised time and again by the opposition's umpire – nasty pasty!

The girls understand. I'm still getting lovely comments about how I look from people, but I still feel horribly nauseated and don't feel very attractive AT ALL. I'm done with the sickness – DONE.

I haven't even had the slightest thought of getting on Keith until I checked the scales and saw that my weight is up. It's doing my head in. I know I'm 12-weeks pregnant, and that you gain weight while you cook up a baby, but because I've been shrinking for so long, growing bigger feels like I am failing and getting fatter again.

The feeling of expanding and always feeling 'full of baby' is like the feeling of being overly full of food. I'm just battling with myself and my hormones I guess.

My nasty old vice called anger

I've thought a lot and have done a whole lot of self-flaying over some bursts of anger and frustration I have succumbed to this week.

First, Lily has been sick – conjunctivitis and vomiting etc. My stress level flew off the scale when she projectile vomited over the couch and I couldn't get the words out of my mouth for Kent to get her off the carpet and onto the tiles QUICKLY.

He yelled at me that he didn't know what I was asking, and I lost it and screamed at him to move the damn child and threw a heavy drink bottle at him at full force. Lily got frightened and was obviously ill, so she started crying and Kent and I dissolved each other with 'I'm going to kill you' glares.

He later said that I have made the last two months hell with my nausea and negativity and that he didn't know what he would have done if the water bottle had hit him. Probably walk out on me is what I thought, just like every other boyfriend has done in the past when I lost the plot.

See where this is going? Old vices are hard to shake, huh? Just when you think you lead a better, more serene, kinder life your old demons rise again.

There's an excellent history in my family of uncontrollable rage and anger layered with plenty of blame of the other person (no matter what). I learnt all the tricks. Blame and never admitting you could be wrong is at the crux of it all.

I played the victim role brilliantly with my previous boyfriends and have had some crazy verbal fights over the years. Kent and I started off that way, then we both mellowed and now generally don't fight, or if we do it's not with raised voices and we often resolve it after a decent conversation and apologies. I don't want our children to see us fight as we did the other day.

Of course, I can see there were a lot of outside influences: hormones, nausea, fear about Lily being sick, stress.... I know they did contribute, but I'm still disappointed in myself for slipping so easily into that manic state.

The second example of anger/frustration this week was in my last game of netball yesterday. We were playing one of the top sides and doing well – staying even or just one down in the scores – then we lost momentum and eventually lost by 17 goals. I felt I was playing a good game and had chatted nicely with my opposition player. I felt puffed, but even when I was getting sandwiched between the GS and GA, I thought that bubba #2 was probably just having the ride of his or her life – swishing around in its amnio fluid and not being hurt at all.

Then we started to really lose, and I got frustrated. My team member, the GD, was picked up for contact outside of the goal ring so I had two girls to defend inside. The GA promptly defended me, so that I couldn't get to the GS, but in doing so she grabbed me around the waist and held onto me (not cool!), and she wasn't picked up for contact by the umpire.

I got pissed off then because they got the pass and as she shot for goal I said, "thanks for the cuddle."

She replied with, "I didn't do anything, I'm just playing netball."

"Well next time," I said, "give us a kiss then too."

By this stage all the players around me and the umpire heard, and the GA was livid with me.

At first I grinned at my wit, but then immediately felt bad and ashamed of myself. I decided to apologise to her after the game, but she refused to shake my hand. I asked their GS to pass on my apologies as I felt I'd been a bad sport.

So then I thanked our umpire and said that it was my last game (he didn't know I was pregnant). He said that I'd had a good season and it was a shame, as he thought I'd played a great game.. He even said he had put me up for best player, but the other umpire said I back-chatted, so dismissed me – KARMA!!

It clarified how I felt. The best games are the ones where you feel you played well and with great positive spirit. Being a good sport is vital. I had fallen into my old vice again of talking back, and it didn't make me feel good at all.

So lessons have been learnt this week; interesting stuff coming up. Maybe I'm missing releasing some energy on Keith and it is building up into anger and frustration.

At least I'm listening to how I would like to react when I am stressed:

I would like to be calm and kind when my children are sick or hurt.

I would like to be respectful at all times when I play netball – to my players, to the opposition and to the umpires.

I especially want my children to do the same when they grow up by learning from my actions.

Please let it be. xxx

This quote struck a chord for me: 'If you are irritated by every rub, how will you ever be polished?'

I like it. I like it a lot.

Beautiful dream

I had a beautiful dream last night. I was sailing a huge sail boat that was more like the size of the titanic. I was surrounded by women, mothers and children and everyone was shrieking with the absolute joy and excitement of the journey. The boat seemed to be decked out with all sorts of different-coloured fabric that had been hand-printed in fabulous designs. The wind was delicious and not strong or cold – sort of like a warm summer's night breeze.

We were moving through big waves and dodging steel ships driven by men, but we easily slipped through all the obstacles and headed toward the coastline that was lit by thousands of gorgeous different-coloured lights of the city. We were in a line of sail boats that were about to land I was nervous that I couldn't do it and we'd crash, but I easily glided to a halt and took down my sail, which was now more like the size of windsurfer. I was alone, but amongst a huge community that were landing amongst the lights on the shore.

It was beautiful. I felt uplifted by the dream. I woke and immediately tried to slip back into that feeling.

Maybe it was about the path to giving birth. Maybe I was being joined by my fellow women spirits.

Just beautiful.

xxx

First pregnancy vs second and beyond

I am envious of my first pregnant-self where I could sit or lie down whenever I needed.

When I was first pregnant:

- I didn't have to keep bending down and picking stuff up off the floor; the floor was as clear as we had left it.
- I didn't have to deal with anything really gross, as I'd whinge to Kent to please deal with it. This time I am in the thick of dirty nappies, mushed up food, snot, cat litter, and stinky cat food.
- I could SLEEP IN if I wasn't working.
- My night's sleep might be interrupted by a pee or two, but not by a crying toddler (3-4 times last night, plus my peeing – sigh).
- I had time to concentrate on the baby growing inside me and thought about it constantly. This time I just try and stop Lily from body-slamming my tummy as much as possible and give my bump a rub hello every night in bed before I drop into a coma.
- My body didn't ache from lifting a giant toddler a thousand times a day.
- I swear the nausea wasn't as soul-destroying as this time.

On the other hand, with a more positive tone. *Now that I am pregnant with my second child:*

- I am nowhere near as scared about having a little baby to care for as I was with my first pregnancy.
- I KNOW that there is a light, and a lovely bottle of Bird in Hand bubbles at the end of the tunnel, and that's the direction I am heading.
- I'm more confident I'll be a good mummy and Kent will be a good daddy.
- I'm looking forward to not making as many 'mistakes' with this baby as I felt I did with Lily in the early days (instead, I'll just make different ones – probably!).
- I have more empathy for mums, as doing this more than once is damn tough – we are strong folk, us women!!
- I am more determined to find myself again after having this child as I'm sure this will be my last child… I'll be ready to rock towards my amazing future.

Just some thoughts.

Have been pretty glum this weekend, so needed to blog. xx

I'm getting better – yay!

I am starting to shake this nausea.

I started to feel a bit better on Tuesday night (when Kent got home) and every day since then I have had more hours in the day when I've been well rather than sick. Now just to get through a whole day without a hint of nausea and I'm popping open a bottle of sparkling apple juice! What a difference. I am hungry, and hungry for good things like veggies and salad and protein etc.

I just did a workout on Keith, and felt good cardio-wise. My fitness it still up there it seems, though my legs, butt, arms, and abs felt it. When Lil has her sleep, I'll jump on Keith again.

I'm looking forward to getting back to cooking. I have a bunch of lovely fruit and veggies from my organic box this week and I'm starting to consider a soup and maybe a veggie casserole/bake thingy – hmmm.

Had a great day shopping up a storm in Kmart on Wednesday. I bought a heap of cute maternity clothes because a) they FIT me, and b) they FIT me!! I also bought Lil some more trackies, shoes etc., and the new bubba some cute white onesies (I was a bit excited in the baby section, which was lovely).

Felt a bit guilty when I got the tally at the checkout, but then I hardly ever go shopping these days and I am being so bloody GOOD in all other areas of my life that a bit of reckless (but lovely and necessary) shopping can be forgiven, surely. I think it's not having my own wage that does it. It's a horrible feeling being 'kept' at times. Oh well, I have another idea brewing re my own business in the future. Maybe one that can create some wealth for us in the future.

Yay to my hormones for finally giving me a break! xx

Secrets

I've just read one blogger's post about how she's kept her operation secret from some of her friends. I was amazed by some comments from her readers who said that she's been dishonest, and they'd feel betrayed if one of their friends didn't tell them if they'd had a Lap Band op.

Just this morning a friend said she was getting a Keith machine and wanted to ask me, apart from exercise, what have I changed food-wise to lose weight. I felt so guilty immediately, but I simply said I haven't worried too much about food; I just have smaller meals and am careful to get enough protein in them (which is true). I didn't want to get caught up on the food side (it tends to lead to shitty dieting talk). Instead, I encouraged her to start exercising if she's keen because she'll hopefully end up loving it like I do.

Driving home I thought what it would be like if my friends ever find out. No doubt some people will be annoyed that I didn't tell them, but you know I am adamant that it is simply MY BUSINESS. I would never judge someone for wanting to keep something private – no matter what it was. Everyone has secrets, even from their closest friends.

I have chosen to tell some dear friends that I know will be discreet, and simply because I know they love me enough not to judge me for it.

I've always been someone who disclosed too much and then felt I had lost ground with some folk because of it. In the last few years I think I've grown enough to feel comfortable with being more private about some things.

I don't know how I'll feel if news about my op ever filters out to the masses, but I'm sure I'll deal with it. And I know if anyone ever confronts me about my silence, I'll feel comfortable enough to look them in the eye and simply say: it's MY BUSINESS. No one else's.

xx

Birth art

I have been reading *Birthing From Within* again, and it suggests you explore your feelings re your baby's birth (past and future).

I thought I'd see what came out re Lily's pregnancy and birth and this is what came up as I created my artwork:

I had a lot of people involved in my pregnancy due to the fact we had IVF initially, my weight impacted where I birthed (which back-up hospital would take me), I had employed an independent midwife, and I still needed to see a separate obstetrician.

To be honest, I had appointments left, right and centre all over Adelaide. The pregnancy was a blur of information, which I was itching for. In hindsight it may have been too much.

I thought by having all the information and assistance I could gather, it would enable me to control the outcome and I would have the gentle homebirth I wanted. Maybe by not letting go enough, I may have had something to do with Lily not 'letting go' and needing to be induced, then helped out?

In my art work, she is saying 'shhh' from the womb. Maybe I didn't listen to my own instincts and to her enough?

I feel that with this pregnancy I want more silence. I want to feel what the baby and I need and go with my instincts. I want less poking and prodding. I want less talking at me. I want to ride the waves of this journey and be more present in each moment.

Lily's birth provided me with shocks to each part of my system. I felt I was in a comic book, being punched at every turn –*KAPOW!*

I don't feel that I was wronged; birth is never black and white, just grey, and that 'punches' are very normal in birth.

I'm glad I had my midwife there to tell me, without any hesitation, that everything that occurred during Lily's birth had to occur due to the medical circumstances. It wasn't my blissful homebirth, it was a full-blown hospitalised emergency c-section. But it had to be that way. Lily and I needed help.

It didn't make me grieve any less. I think I am still very sad at times, but that is ok; I can be sad.

I'm not quite sure how it has made me feel about this impending baby's birth.

I now know that I will not have control – what will be, will be.

It may be a perfect VBAC (vaginal birth after c-section) at our local hospital with just the midwives attending me (best-case scenario), but it may end up like Lily's birth with much confusion and a c-section. I can't change the outcome.

I don't want special music, fairy lights and a room of support people this time. I'm not too fussed about a birth plan and I'm certainly not going to rule out pain medication if required. I just want Kent and I to get on with it in peace, with a good supportive presence of midwives and doctors if necessary.

I know that once the birth is over, the punches don't end there. I know the first few weeks with a newborn is bloody hard work, so I want to conserve some energy for that time too.

The art was an interesting process. It made me aware of needing to guard myself a bit more through this pregnancy and to let go more at the baby's birth.

Let's see what happens. xxx

Patience

My patience is being tested BIG time today. Lily has not slept during the day other than a half hour in the car, and she has persistently cried — her long moaning wail that makes me want to walk out the door and drive far, far away. I'm not sure why I'm being tested today. I woke feeling shattered and very sick in the tummy.

Bruce the cat has decided to get on the bandwagon too and wail at me when Lily isn't — for food he knows he's not going to get until the evening. I have then had to struggle against ferocious winds and horizontal rain to get wood for the fire. One piece of wood has just driven a splinter into my soft hands that aren't equipped for manual labour. THAT'S IT! I want to get off this fucking ride and be by myself — feeling well and not in pain.

What the hell am I going to do when I have a baby and a miserable toddler to look after when Kent is working away? Where do I find the patience to get through a day like this with a newborn to top it off? Why the hell am I here, being a mother when I had a simple, free life?

I want to be at the pub with the netballers drinking after our final game; cold from the game but being warmed by wine and camaraderie.

I miss being ME.

So now after that rant, I start to consider what I can feed Lily for dinner that won't make me throw up, and I contemplate her going to bed at 6.30pm and me following at 7pm. Fuck this Saturday 14th of August 2010. I'm over it.

A new diet that works

So I found a new diet that allows you to shed 3.6kgs in 24-48 hours and it's called Squirty Bum!

My Saturday got a whole lot worse through the night and all Sunday and all last night.

Today I am shaky, have weak limbs and haven't eaten since Saturday night.

The runs on top of pregnancy and nausea is THE BOMB – literally.

My folks got home yesterday but not in time to save me, and Kent is going to arrive home tomorrow night after the devastation has passed.

Lily had the bug with less drama at the end of last week, so I hope that this critter remains with me and doesn't get passed on to anyone.

I'm going to try some juice and toast first to feed the bump (I simply can't be bothered for myself). Bubs has been kicking away brilliantly the whole time.

Now back to moaning and panting through my mouth to make me feel better – yuck.

Blessings. x

Appease

I am getting over the bug it seems. Feeling much more myself today, which includes the ever-present pregnancy nausea (it's sort of like a guest that has overstayed its welcome – you were happy to see it at first because it meant the pregnancy was going well, but now it frankly just needs to leave!). Then again, I've acknowledged it as part of me – to an extent – and definitely part of my journey. I think this is why:

Last night I was tucked up in bed reading *Eat, Pray, Love* and it spoke of choosing words to summarise a place or yourself. Out of nowhere APPEASE came into my mind. At first, I felt I was being downtrodden if I needed to appease other people, but then I realised that it came from love for myself. I am appeasing myself through this period of my life where I need to 'bring it to a state of peace or quiet – calm'.

I am so agitated at times by the halt in what I saw as progress in my life that I forget that this, too, is a time for growth and development. Yes, it's damn tough, but that's what it takes sometimes.

I am appeasing myself through this period of nausea and the physical and emotional aspects of this pregnancy. I am appeasing my body's need to remain healthy and fit through exercise and a balanced diet as much as possible in my ill state. I am appeasing my racing mind by blogging and journaling and constantly reviewing.

One thing that appeases me the most is looking at my life and noting what I have manifested so far. I can't believe how wonderful my life is compared to how I was feeling about it four to five years ago.

Today I am blessed with all of this:

Spirituality: My sense of the divine is ever-present and brings me eternal peace and love. It embraces and shapes all aspects of my life below.

Home/Family: I have a very comfortable sanctuary at home, a beautiful marriage, wonderful child(ren) and much more healthy relationships with my relatives.

Health: I have achieved some weight-loss and an increased level of fitness. We eat well, including local, organic fruit and veg.

Wealth: We're paying off our debts and I am learning to be thrifty, which is a wonderful feeling.

Self: Self-love and acceptance is getting easier. I am also proud of my relationships with friends and others.

Work/Dreams: I'm not *having* to work, which is amazing and a blessing that I often forget. My future paid-working path can actually be anything I want it to be. How wonderful is that?! My dreams are forever being created and whirling around, bringing me to the place I need to be.

So today I am in a better place. May this positivity last.

Blessings. xx

Health = happiness

It's not until you lose your health that you understand just how precious it is.

I have just got through 12 weeks straight of pregnancy nausea and now I am well again.

It is AMAZING!! xx

My body is dancing with joy at all the new taste sensations I'm now enjoying.

It sings for freshly-made coleslaw with herbs from the garden and lemon juice. It's delighting in tuna sandwiches and steak – different proteins besides just cheese and nuts.

My brain is switching back on and I am feeling excited about cooking, cleaning and organising (i.e. nesting).

My energy levels are increasing with each decent meal and good night's sleep.

I am basically just damn HAPPY!

I've had a great week with Kent being home (though I miss him now).

Life is just GREAT.

Can't say much more than that.

Hope your life is great, too!

Blessings. xx

Day dreaming

I've caught myself at least a hundred times in the last two days, day dreaming about where I'd like to be besides here. My reality is that I am up to my wrists in pooey nappies, busy wiping mushed avocado and watermelon off the high chair for the seventh time in a row, or that I'm wrestling toddler legs into, out of, or up onto something. Miss Lily has been extra noisy too, just vocalising in the car, whining for something out of her reach, or just banging shit around.

My patience is really being tried.

I am dreaming of holidays – decadent hotel rooms, drinking champers in a lounge bar, floating in a warm pool, just chatting to Kent over dinner, even lying in bed and reading without waiting for the baby to wake up.

I never knew how much freedom I had before I had Lily. What WAS I thinking??!! lol

Then again, when she comes over to me with her huge smiling eyes and gives me a spontaneous kiss and then giggles, my heart melts.

The holiday will wait. My daydreams are always free and they're there for me to tap into in my mind whenever I want.

Think I'm about to head to Fiji and sit on a beach as she's grabbing at my keyboard for the twentieth time.

Serenity now!!!

Dear Chloe

Father's Day has brought about connection with Kent's adult daughter, Chloe. I feel I need to write to her, though I'm not sure if I'll ever send this to her.

Dear Chloe,

I've never written to you, but I've had some of these conversations with you in my head for years now.

Hello, to you: the lovely, first-born daughter of my love, Kent. Seeing your recent photo is amazing as I see so much of Kent and his family in you. I think I can see some wicked, happy-go-lucky spirit in you and I can imagine us all having so many laughs together. I have never written to, or journalled about you as I've always thought that I might intrude on that personal space that you and your dad are establishing. I would never want to influence your relationship with him by my noted thoughts – written by a bystander, to somewhat of degree. Though, in saying that, I feel more than that already. You are part of our little family – me, Kent, our two children and you – their sister.

I am so proud of Kent for getting in contact with you. It took a lot of courage for him to do so. It has taken you possibly even more courage to do the same. I think the timing of Kent's contact with you is special as I have seen him grow since I met him eight years ago – he has now grown into a beautiful father to Lily and in doing so, he is also growing more into his role as your dad.

I know there have been many years and important events in your life he hasn't experienced with you but he now has the opportunity to know you as the woman you are now. You will no doubt establish a friendship and ease with each other over time and it will become your special relationship – unique just to you two. You and your sister and ? will also have your own special relationships as siblings and this will grow over the years.

From me to you, though, Chloe – as a gal, who can remember not long ago being 20 (I'm only 16 years older, but gee it feels like five minutes ago!), and who has friends in their early 20s, I hope that we get an opportunity to become friends. I can already imagine us going out together maybe for lunch and a bit of shopping and then finishing up with a drink at the pub and maybe a few silly dances around the jukebox.

Who knows where this could go for us all.

I don't know if I'll ever send this to you because I don't know if I have the guts to just yet.

Sometimes the thought of you coming into our life makes me nervous – but then I realise that I have nothing to fear as you can only add more love to our lives. Welcome to you, the lovely Ms Chloe.

Hope this is the start of something fabulous.

Much Love, Ailsa.

Touching base

Life has been happily busy with Kent home quite a lot and a mini trip to his hometown for a wedding.

I'm 20 weeks pregnant now – halfway and I'm feeling great! Just a bit tired, which is usual, but apart from that I still hardly feel pregnant.

My bump is growing, but I am still 'neat' as someone described me. Bubba is very busy moving around, and we had news yesterday about whether it is a 'pink' or 'blue' bubba.

Unfortunately, I cannot tell ANYONE as I have sworn myself to secrecy and intend on sticking to it. Kent keeps telling me that it might not be 100% accurate anyway, so not to get it too stuck in my mind what we're having. The excitement of knowing the gender was a bit marvellous yesterday, but today it's faded a little. Yesterday, it felt a bit like I was driving to give birth because that's what I was thinking the whole way down to the hospital to have Lily – is it going to be a boy or girl??!!

Anyhoo, the main thing is that the baby is growing perfectly and that all is well as far as I know from the scan (I'll see the OB on Friday to confirm). I had a million comments at the wedding re how well I looked from people who haven't seen me since I had the operation. It got a bit overwhelming, but fortunately due to the pregnancy I was able to steer conversations away from weight-loss (how I've done it, how much I've lost etc.,) to how I'm feeling carrying this baby – phew!

Selective with my heart

Kick-a-dah, kick-a-dah, kick.... Hello, lovely baby! I know you are there just saying 'hi' to your mummy, but I'm trying to concentrate on blogging here!

What to say? Life is still grand! Yay!

I had an appointment with my Band specialist GP last week, and she was so pleased for me because the baby is growing perfectly, and I'm maintaining my weight – awesome!

I then saw my OB, who is blunt and not nearly as endearing, but even he was pleased with my weight. He said I have a few kilos to play with (put on if I need to). It seemed he was finally interested in how I must feel so many kgs lighter than when I fell pregnant with Lil.

"You can't imagine," I simply said to him.

And that's just it – he *can't* imagine, being a lean, 60-something-year-old man.

I didn't feel the need to go into any details with him because he wasn't interested previously in how I felt about being sent to all sorts of different doctors in a different hospital because I was too 'obese' and might break a local hospital bed when giving birth to Lily. Hmph!!

I'm getting stronger in maintaining boundaries, and only opening up to the right sort of people these days. Not that I want to become withdrawn, just selective and graceful when I disclose things close to my heart.

Home alone(ish)

Kent left for work early this morning, so Lily and I are on our own for 12 days.

What to do, besides being a bit weepy and sitting around with Lil in our dressing gowns eating fruit toast? I know... blog! Then clean, then probably blog a bit more.

First a gorgeous moment from last week:

Lily is in her brand new 'big girl bed', which she has thankfully taken to beautifully bar a little visit last night. I found a little girl walking in her sleeping bag toward our room at 12.45pm... she'd worked out how to: a) get out of bed, and b) master walking in a sleeping bag in the dark. Clever cat!

I did exactly what you aren't supposed to do and popped her straight into our bed (she was a little chilly – my excuse anyway), and she proceeded to keep both Kent and I awake for about 20 minutes before I moved her back to her bed. I have to admit, though, the divine gentle sweeps of her warmed little hands on the nape of my neck to check where her mummy was just made me melt. If you bottled the intense love you can feel for your children, it would heal the world, surely?!

Misplaced Daddy

Lily keeps asking after her Daddy, but I think she kinda understands that he's just away temporarily. Occasionally she asks if he is maybe in the shower or the shed like we've just misplaced him for a bit – ha ha!

I can imagine the reunion next week will be a bit EXCITING for both of them.

Ms Perfect can piss off

Well, well... I'm cramming a bit of tomato on toast down as I've forgotten to eat today – tut, tut.

It's not my fault really, it's the crazy, pregnant, Ms Perfect alter ego I have. See, she likes to clean, *really* clean (behind stuff even?!) and she is relentless, often not stopping for a pee! She is sort of my version of Alice from the TV show *The United States of Tara*, but she doesn't dress as well.

Today, in fact, she is in a pair of ¾ stretch bike pants. Two words come to mind – turkey drumsticks (or is that three words?). All I can say if I happen to come to the door for you wearing them... LOOK AWAY!!!! I've warned you.

Anyway, I have decided to tell my Ms Perfect Alice to piss off because today I found her on top of a stool cleaning the top of the fridge for Christ's sake. She is taking over my day-to-day life a bit whilst Kent is away. Must remind myself that it can be unhealthy and to sit down at times and relax!

Vent over.

My old jeans

Skewed reality

I helped my mum tidy up my old room at my parents' house the other day.

I was hoping to unearth some old pieces of clothing I left behind prior to leaving home.

I remember that 20-year-old girl setting off for sunny Queensland with a dream of letting many unhealthy things go, including my recent ex-boyfriend and a heap of weight. I didn't realise that I would get incredibly homesick and gain weight. My solace was food – takeaways plus Bundaberg Rum and coke. When I returned home, friends asked what had happened; they were visibly shocked at my appearance. Needless to say, the weight gain didn't end there, and I steadily gained more and more until I hit my top weight.

One image has permeated my conscience throughout my struggle with weight, and that is of my wonderful flippy, spotty dress. Mum bought it for me when I was 16-17 and I wore it to death for a few summers before it became too small for me. I have memories of turning boys' heads in that dress, of having long, tanned legs and a twirl in my step. Well, my mother kept it for me. It is not just a memory, it is now a reality again and boy can memories get skewed. It is just a dress, a navy spotty, *large*, Esprit dress.

It just goes to show that that girl with a swinging step and long tanned legs had curves and knew that she looked healthy and good. Something for me to remember as I move on with my weight-loss once I've had the bubba. Watch this space for a pic of me twirling in the spotty dress next year!

And yes, I have tried it on already, but it doesn't quite look the same with a baby bump; more like a knocked-up teenager!

Besides THE dress, I also came across two pairs of jeans from that same time – my late teens. They were with a note that said: *"Please send up to Qld when I'm thin again"*.

Bless that gorgeous young goddess who thought she was too big even then. My motherly goddess self – 15 years on – wraps love around her and tells her that she is just perfect the way she is, and that jean technology will come a long way in 15 years; stretch, dark denim is WAY more flattering!

Hindsight is a wonderful thing, huh?

Now I just need to find that white halter neck top that made men's eyes pop out of their heads and I'd be set! Ha, ha!

Thankfully that lil ditty was binned long ago!

It was DANGEROUS! Ba ha ha! xxxx

It's a sad affair

Sat night – check

Home already after a 'rocking' night out for dinner at my folks – check.

Milo consumed – check.

Toddler asleep – check.

Want to get to sleep before 10pm – check.

Sitting in a silent house tapping away at the computer – check.

It's a sad affair this pregnant, sometimes single, mummy life of mine.

Zooming ahead 12 months, please let my life be a bit more fun… PLEASE?!

Blessings. xx

Nip, nip, woof, woof

I have been well and truly chomped on by the black dog today.

My body is telling me to sit the hell down and eat carbs on the lounge.

I am feeling really heavy from the pregnancy and just terribly sad.

The next month is going to be a test. Kent has been away for 12 days and back for two, now he's gone again (for two weeks) and the next time he's back home he's going away on a motorbike trip for the weekend. So effectively Lily and I see him for two nights in the next month.

I don't begrudge him the trip away because I know he looks forward to it every year and I know he's working long hours for us as a family, it's just hard being the one left at home.

I think the most frustrating thing is that after feeling that I've progressed so far in my life and have evolved so much, I realise I am still basing much of my happiness on attachment to another person – my partner.

Today I'm wondering what my life is 'for' when all I am doing is longing for the company of Kent. When he's away I'm simply filling in time until he gets back. I am well-versed with Lennon's line: 'Life is what happens while you're busy making other plans'... and looking back on moments that have brought real happiness in my life, often Kent has not been there for one reason or another.

Mostly, of course, my days shine when he's by my side, especially when we have many indulgent conversations reliving something adorable or funny our Miss Lily has done.

I guess I am still in the position of waiting for this bubba to arrive, too. My life is in limbo in more ways than one, and no doubt will be until our children move out of home!

So today I do my best with a bad day. I acknowledge it for what it is. I slept when Lily napped and didn't get out of my pjs until 1pm today. I'm eating those carbs my body is craving and am about to sit on the lounge for a while.

Tomorrow is a new day and just might feel a bit better than today.

Hope you are enjoying some of the sunshine outside.

Blessings. xx

Operation crap myself because Christmas is coming and so is this baby!

13-14 weeks till the baby is here. Fark, fark, fark!!

Christmas will be here in eight weeks and you know what that means – time decides to speed up before and after.

I have a heap of jobs I want to get done before the birth and have hardly started on them.

Are you hearing me, Kent? Panicked pregnant woman here – heeeeeeelllp!!

So, I'll do what I do best when stressed. I'll make myself a to-do list.

Well, six lists later and I'm feeling a bit better.

Now just to start getting through them.

Today is 'start in the baby's room' day as it has turned into a dumping ground. Wish me luck!

BTW, had a few nice Mummy Moments yesterday. I was feeding Lily her bottle of milk in the morning and she got all snuggly and zoned out while she drank and played gently with her hair. I was remembering her feeding from me and thought that I'm glad I'll get the chance to breastfeed the new bubba. Having them suckle and gently move their little hands around while they feed is so divine. Awww.

I'm starting to also consider that as a youngish pregnant woman I am the embodiment of health and new life really, so I should embrace this wonderful phase as it will pass so quickly.

I also got to thinking about Christmas 2010. This year, even though I am again waiting for another big change to occur in my life with the birth of my second child, I am confident in my mothering skills and I am feeling so much healthier. So bring on the fa, la, la, las, decorations and Christmas goodies – I'm going to enjoy myself this year!

Not a pretty swan in my books

Kent has come and gone over night. Keeping my chin up, I've decided to do nice things for us this weekend to pass the time.

Lily and I had a lovely morning at swimming and because the weather is so damn good today I decided to grab us some snacks from the organic market and head to the Adelaide Hills botanic gardens for a while.

It was simply stunning, as always, and Lil and I enjoyed our juice and muffin on a rug on the grass. Then I suggested we go and look at the duckies – big mistake!

We wandered down to the lake and as we did a group of about 30-odd older ladies were crossing the path above the lake. I heard a few ahhs as Lily happily chased a little ducky down to the water. He was keen for some food, but not a chase – so off he went. Then along came an army of other ducks and a *mother* of a black swan heading directly toward me and Lil. Lily promptly went around them and proceeded to the water while the evil swan started to rear up at me and spread it wings – FARK!!

I am not good with birds, particularly chickens or roosters because of a feisty rooster experience as a kid, so you can imagine my reaction to this bloody huge, nasty swan – arghhhhh! The only thing stopping me from running was, of course, Lily. My mother instincts kicked in and I was seriously ready to wallop the thing if it came between me and Lily. But the group of women were clucking about the damn swan, and Lily had entered the lake by now.

Quick thinking made me grab what was left of our gorgeous lemon-and-poppyseed muffin and hoick some away from the swan. It took the bait, so I grabbed Lil before she got up to her knees in the lake. When I turned around, the fucker was back, so I threw more muffin away from it and scrambled up the bank to where the women were saying: "Oh, that was a nasty swan wasn't it!" and "My goodness, I hope those aren't good shoes she's wearing!" pointing to Lil'.

Composure still held, I said the shoes will dry and yes, it was a pretty mean swan; not that the bugger nearly got a punch in the beak with my full bag if it had gone anywhere near my gal.

So next time, fuck the ducks! We'll stick with the grass thanks, and I'll be sure to keep my eye out for any swan/geese/other nasty, evil birds when out and about.

Fight

After a fight re babysitting with my parents...

Why is everything so conditional with the pair of you? Why can't you see what I need and hear me when I am stressed? Why can't Kent be home to help me here instead of me having to rely on my fucking parents for help?

Why am I alone, crying tears onto my keyboard on a Saturday night? Why is it always my responsibility to look after Lily?

I'm angry at everyone. I am sad for myself and Lily.

I hope Lily is calmer and happier tomorrow; she is no doubt picking up on all the drama and it is manifesting itself in her full-on behaviour.

Morning contemplation

I'm feeling emotionally bruised this morning; puffy-eyed and knackered... but ok.

Life will go on.

Mum sent me a text explaining that they of course love Lily, and she wasn't bad (that part I know, as she's only a damn child!!), she was just revved up.

I've chosen not to reply for now.

I'm just here, doing my best. I am trying to look after the property, the house, the arrangements for the new baby, Lily, and myself mostly alone.

I've had 28 days in the last few weeks without Kent being home, therefore 28 days of complete responsibility and possibly another 14 to come. No wonder I'm feeling a bit stressed.

So back to today: a new, fresh day – thank goodness.

Lily is happy and smiling. We're off to a local kindy fete to see friends and buy cake. Then later today I plan on us having a great afternoon sleep and then maybe relax with a movie. Bugger outside influences; Lil, Bubs and I can do just fine by ourselves.

Blessings. xx

P.S. My dad just rode his bike up to us and said that he loved both Lily and I and was sorry that it ended up so badly last night. I explained that Lil and I are both probably feeling the pressure of being without Kent and that our communication breakdown was the issue last night. All is well anyway. We'll sort it out. Ah the joys of family…

Letting go

This week has been a bit emotional.

I'm ok now, just feeling things a bit more distinctly… like I am really switched on.

I have sent my letter of resignation into work. My unpaid parental leave ceases in December and I gave notice that I wouldn't be returning due to the impending birth of our second child. As I wrote it, I knew it was the right thing to do and that that period of my life is over. As I was driving to post the letter, I began to feel a bit uneasy. Posting it meant that I no longer had any backup of my own if anything went wrong. My employment was MY OWN – it didn't rely on anyone (i.e. Kent or my parents). *I got my job and I made my own success.* I could financially support myself, even Kent and I when he began his business. Now I am absolutely reliant on Kent to pay for me and our children.

I know this has been the case for nearly two years now, but posting that final letter saying to give my position to someone else was hard. I am having to really let go and trust that when the time is right, I will again be able to enter the workforce and be successful in my career. Feelings about money and being reliant on my parents as a student have reared their ugly heads. I know this is different – I am not 'sponging' off Kent, I am working damn hard as a mother. I just need to let go of some of those worries and TRUST.

I had an orientation at the hospital yesterday, which went really well. I felt informed of most things already from Lil's birth, but I was keen to check out the birthing bath/pool in case I get a chance to have a water birth. It was great to get my head around where it will all take place, and I started feeling a bit excited to meet this little one after listening to newborn cries coming from the rooms.

The only thing I wasn't prepared for was the trigger of the smells in the hospital, in particular the maternity ward. It was like I was zoomed back to the first few days of Lily's life where we were in shambles! She just wouldn't stop crying and I was having so much trouble feeding her, let alone getting around after the c-section and trying to look a bit 'with it' for visitors.

The smell is pretty horrible, really. A mix of cooking and medicine. Anyway, I thought to myself that I will endeavour to change my memories of the smell by having a much better experience this time. Then again, if it all goes pear-shaped, I know that life will go on and the tough parts will pass! Phew for prior knowledge, huh?!

The staff were just gorgeous. Many of the midwives are familiar to me and I'll have my midwife with me the whole time.

So here's to feeling emotions, letting go, and trusting that *all will be well*…

Blessings. xxx

Food epiphany

I had an epiphany last night whilst watching *Junior Masterchef* and watching the judges eat an impressive dessert with gusto. That pure sense of joy when you experience good food is a wonder of life, isn't it?!

I now know that in the past I would have thought about eating that dessert and emotions of guilt would instantly surface for me – I'd do it anyway and probably overeat to stuff some of that guilt down. But now, I simply don't *feel scared* of food. It might sound ludicrous, but that's what I was… scared of food and all that was wrapped up emotionally in it for me. Now it is simply a pleasure, and mostly small portions of GREAT food is what makes my heart sing. How liberating. Is this how 'normal' people feel about food?! Is it as simple as that? Wow – hope so.

Blessings. xxx

Kent, Lily and Chloe

Post-Sydney trip wrap-up

After months now of Kent and his eldest daughter Chloe reconnecting via letters and over the phone, we went to visit her in Sydney. It was the first time I'd met Chloe, and many years since Kent had seen her. We met her, her boyfriend and her aunt in Sydney. It was a bit nerve-wracking waiting for them to arrive at Darling Harbour, but when they did we soon fell into relaxed banter after lots of hello kisses and hugs.

Lily was the centre of attention (as all toddlers are), and Chloe and Lily really enjoyed playing with each other. Chloe had a new doll for Lil, which she adores, and we went off and had coffee, then a shop, then some lunch and finally a cuppa back at our apartment. Nothing was awkward, we were all laughing a lot, so the conversation was friendly and easy the whole time.

Chloe is Kent's eldest daughter and a lovely, bubbly, kind-hearted 20 year old who, from what I saw, was simply feeling excited, but also a bit nervous about meeting her dad and his family after so long. We've made plans to meet again next year with Kent's family. I can imagine that it has brought up many emotions for her meeting with us, as it has for Kent. I'm feeling happy, but also relieved that our catch up went well. I feel protective over Chloe and feel like I have made a new young friend, like one of my younger netball girlfriends. Kent obviously has much deeper feelings, but I think he finds it hard to put it into words.

Anyway, we've been blessed with a great outcome so far. I hope Chloe feels the same.

Since getting back, Kent has had to fly back out to work for 10-ish days.

I'm very glad to be on home turf as I am getting more and more Braxton Hicks, and have that internal mother's urge to stay close to home – just in case!

Cats

Miss Lily is becoming better friends with the puss-cats. I caught Ned with her snuggling on the couch today.

Then tonight after her bath she propped herself up on the 'pillas' (her way of saying pillows) and then both Ned and Bruce joined her in a group snuggle.

I think she's going to be one hell of an animal lover like me. She might get caught talking to chickens in a coup one day and saying, "it's ok, don't be afraid... I'm not a monster".

My Aunty Jill tells that story about me over and over. I'm sure I'll have plenty of stories like that about Lil. *cute*

Lily with Ned the cat

Need things to be 'straight'

The other night I had a lot of pain (period like pain) and couldn't sleep. I had a panic attack that it was early labour and I wasn't organised, so the next day I got myself completely sorted.

Kent is going back to work until just before Christmas Day and then hopefully be home for good after that (though I write that with huge trepidation!).

My body and mind are screaming for him to just come home and stay put! It feels like I can't settle down and get psychologically ready for this baby until he is here with me to do the same. I can't do it all by myself, I need his focus on this new little soul entering our life too.

So here's to a bit of help from the gorgeous Universe to assist things to fall into place for me quickly and easily. Help me get 'straight' and rested prior to our beautiful bubba's birth. In the meantime, I will aim to let go and remember that *what will be, will be.*

Blessings. xxx

Lily's 1st Christmas with my dad, her Puppa Geoff.

Giving thanks at Christmas time

I wish to give thanks for all aspects of my life because I am truly blessed.

I give thanks for:

My best friend, Kent, who supports all that I wish to be and all that I already am. His love helps me soar, but also keeps me grounded. Our laughter rings out throughout the house whenever we are together. He makes me feel so loved and special. He is a gentle, unassuming but doting father. I've seen him blossom this year as a daddy and as a successful project manager. I'm very, very proud of him, and to be his wife.

Our beautiful girl Lily. I never believed that you can love like this before I became a mother. My heart could explode in beams of light with all the happiness she brings into our lives. I am privileged to watch her develop into her own little person – full of spirit, empathy, humour and joy. She will no doubt astound us when she becomes an older sister, but I'm glad to have had two full years of just concentrating on and loving her.

Our new amazing bubba. The anticipation of his or her arrival is blissful and intoxicating. Less fear and more knowledge of the intense joy of a child is raising both Kent and I up. Every flutter in my belly sends waves of love to my heart.

Our families who are supportive, gentle and loving to us. We have learnt so much from them all and we are so lucky to have such close relationships.

Baby Lily with my mother in law, her Nanna June.

Our friends who are spread far and wide and who come from all sorts of times in our lives, but who all contribute to our world and our happiness. Kent and I have talked about how blessed we are to love and be loved by so many different folk. It's been important for us to reflect on this with the loss of our dear mate Peg recently. It's important to touch people's lives gently and respectfully, accepting them for all that they are. If you don't feel that someone is doing the same for you, then let them go and surround yourself with people that lift you up.

I'd like to give extra thanks for my beautiful readers and dear friends. You are inspirational to me. I write to you almost daily knowing you are quietly supporting me through every step of my life. Without you as gentle sounding boards, I'd probably have gone a little mad this past year, being stuck home alone on the hill with a toddler. Thank you, thank you! xx

The Universe for blessing us with abundance in all forms. We do not *want* for anything. Our hearts are filled with love, our home is bursting with laughter and joy.

For Christmas and being able to share its magic with Lily this year. Our tree is so pretty, the gifts surrounding it full of anticipation of how they'll light up the receiver's face, the music is soothing, and the festive spirit is giddying. I aim to approach Christmas Day with grace, patience and joy, and to revel in all of its glorious touches, letting the not-so-glorious moments fade away.

My health. I am lighter today (minus the baby bump) than I was last year. I can move differently. I eat gorgeous meals and I rejoice in every morsel without guilt. My body is healthier, and my mind is much less toxic. I am loving myself, and every part of me, more.

Making my long-term dreams come true. I am honestly blessed with the manifestation of dreams I have been dreaming of for many, many years.

The sky really is the limit, if there are indeed any limits on what blessings you can receive from the Universe.

May I always remember my blessings and give thanks for all the abundance in our lives. May those around me also have all their wishes come true and that they find their own way to give thanks for what they already have.

All is well in our world – mwah! xx

2011

MOTHERING / MOVEMENT / JUGGLING / LONESOME

Nesting – Just a quickie before I hit the lounge and relax

The nesting has continued and I'm afraid I may have given the bug to Kent because he's been an absolute darling and scrubbed, cleaned and dusted the life out of the house with me. Actually, I've been organising things and he's been the one doing the hard labour (pardon the pun – lol).

I've taken a couple of pics of him vacuuming the blinds in the kitchen and changing/cleaning the light fittings. He's also been up scrubbing the mould on the bathroom ceiling (from the dryer in winter) while I had a nap.

All this, along with looking after Miss Lily 90% of the time, well, what can I say??? What a man!!!! I love you, baby! Thank you sooooo much.

It's been a busy time and yes, I've been doing too much, but it's also been a happy time getting ready for this new bubba. I'm getting very excited now!

The baby is fully engaged, but according to my OB this means nothing apparently. It certainly FEELS like something! I'm happy to birth any time after Sunday now, so when you're ready little one, Mummy is too! xx

Lily kissing my pregnant belly

Made it to 37 weeks

Yay! I have passed the 37-week mark. Now I'm ready to rock!! Bring on the birth! lol!

Baby capsule fitted in car – check. Eyebrows waxed – check. Lap Band deflated – check. I am good to birth! lol

It seems I've made it through all my important appointments this week without going into labour. Great... now bring it on.

I am carrying on about getting this birth underway now, and again forgetting that Divine timing will just have to do its thing. This baby will decide when it arrives, not me. Patience and Acceptance will again be my lessons. Oh bugger... te he!

And then if I'm still waiting for this baby (it could be for up to three weeks yet), then I may possibly go out of my mind with lack of sleep, excitement and anticipation. Last night I had a *glorious* hourly ritual of going to the loo through the night – 11pm, 12, 1, 2, 3 – then a break till 6am with a million flips and groans between – blurgh.

My eyes are barely slits this morning, but thankfully Miss Lily has been dropped off to childcare by Kent, and the day is mine (ours) – yay.

So it's been a year – wow

Thursday came and went without much fuss. One year since my Band op.

I suppose it has just become a part of me and my life now.

One thing that jumped into my sloppy mind is that nowdays when I see someone cycling past me up a hill, or running, or doing any form of exercise where they are exerting themselves I feel excited for them and jealous that I am not getting their buzz. Prior to my weight-loss, I'd feel just downright guilty and miserable that I wasn't, and sometimes couldn't, do what they're doing. That desire to move my body is such a wonderful gift, one that I remember as a child and young person and it's BACK!

Speaking of feeling like I did in the past, that's really how I feel now. The true, authentic Ailsa who is more confident in her body, healthier, and wants to move her limbs and dance and laugh every day. I will eternally give thanks for reconnecting with myself. xx

Yesterday we had another gorgeous day. After a late start we headed down to the beach near my Gramp's home. I spent lots of time on that beach as a child, so I was reliving wonderful memories whilst watching Lily. We all collected magical shells and rocks and Kent found us a few shells with holes in them ready to make them into necklaces. I've always looked for those shells, so when we got home and he made Lily and I necklaces, he just spoke to my soul. I love him so much for those necklaces. Lily wanted to wear hers to bed, bless her. xx

We then packed up and had a yummy lunch at a Greek restaurant. Lily was so good, even though she was dead tired. She sat up on her own adult chair and had a cloth napkin on her lap. She gobbled up taramasalata, eggplant and skordalia dip, then enjoyed calamari and copied her mummy by squeezing lemon on hers – hilarious!

We ordered some chips for her, but she was more than happy to eat all the other dishes. I was so proud of her trying everything. As kids, my brother and I loved going to a Greek restaurant with our parents, so yesterday's meal brought back more wonderful childhood memories.

The sun, the sand, the salt, the love, the memories and the magic made the day a diamond for me. Today I feel almost buffed-up by the elements and love and I'm feeling very, very calm.

I'm still cookin', good lookin'

This baby is still cooking away. We saw the OB yesterday, and the baby has plenty of fluid around it, and is happy and calm in there. I am well, and my blood pressure is good. The baby hasn't come right down though yet, and my cervix hasn't dilated apparently; therefore, any sort of inducing is out of the question.

Needless to say, I was disappointed. I was, however, pleased that the OB admitted that some women carry their babies to 42 weeks comfortably – it's natural for some. He seems to think my body likes to cook my babies a little longer than 40 weeks (not many seem to consider this fact).

He was happy to wait another week and see me next Friday. He doesn't seem to think much will change in that week, but of course anything can happen. He did offer to pencil me in for a c-section the following Monday if I wished, but he wasn't at all pushy – he simply gave me the option.

I have agreed to be tentatively booked in on Monday the 7th of Feb. I just need to have an end-date in my head, otherwise I'm going to go mad.

Swear words

Lily is so cute! She knows how to say 'cheese' now and pose for the camera. Oh, and the not so cute part? She knows the word 'shit', and how to put it into context, e.g. when she knocked something over the other day and said, "shit". I corrected her with 'oh dear', so then she said, "shit, oh dear". It was so hard not to laugh!! Whoops!

Lily in the garden

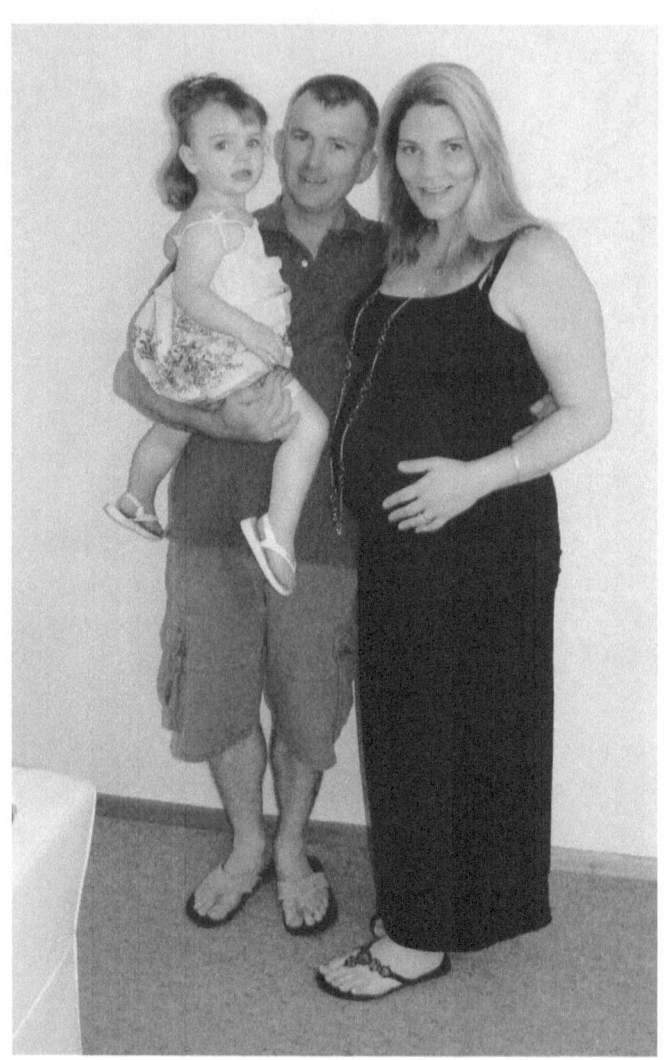

Our family of three, plus a bump.

One more sleep!

There was no change in the baby's position Friday, and labour hasn't started itself (yet), so looks like we'll be meeting our baby at 8am tomorrow morning – how EXCITING!!!!

And that means only one more sleep in this enormous state, with cankles, itchy feet, and my bottom lip sticking out – lol.

So today I complete my packing and lists and in between I'll cuddle my gal, as I'm going to miss being with her the next week.

Still can't believe I'm going to be holding our baby in my arms tomorrow. It feels so surreal.

So today I farewell my pregnant self for the final time as I don't ever intend on having more children. I'm proud of my body throughout this pregnancy for being such a wonderful space for my growing bub. It's obviously cosy inside there!

Our family of four with baby Tess.

Welcome to the world baby Tess!

Baby Tess was born at 8.47am 7th February, 2011.

It was a joyful, peaceful birth. She is divine, and we are so very, very happy.

We are blessed with another goddess – go girl power!! I am going to raise sisters, how exciting!

Tess' birth went exactly as planned. I walked into the theatre with my own gown on and one nurse commented that I was glowing. I felt calm, happy, and so excited. She was born into an audience of happy, bubbly medical staff and midwives. Van Morrison's *Moondance* was playing at some stage, and there was often bursts of laughter amongst the group.

Kent was carefully avoiding being in the way of the medical staff, but he was right by my side. Tess arrived big, healthy, and loudly like her sister. She instantly calmed as she was placed against my neck and chest. It was so natural to have her in front of me. She wasn't a surprise. It was like she had been in my life forever already. Tess is a born attacher; she got straight onto my floppy breasts and filled her belly before lying blissfully on me. Such a clever, clever girl!

My pain after the op was at times pretty nasty, but nothing unbearable. I have healed well, I think. I still have twinges almost three weeks on, but that's probably because I am doing too much, as usual.

My parents brought Lily out to meet Tess in the afternoon of Day 1. She was so, so excited! We gave her a t-shirt saying 'Big Sister Lily', telling her it was from Tess. She wasn't jealous at all, just enormously revved up.

So we made it through Day 1.

By the next morning I was up and about and managed to have a tentative shower. Tess was basically breastfeeding or sleeping on the job 24/7, otherwise she was crying. As I couldn't stand up and rock her for long periods to soothe her, I had to either feed her or try a dummy, which I cautiously pulled out of my bag. A few of the midwives showed their dismay at that, but others understood my dilemma. Being my second child, I felt empowered to tell people that I *was* going to use a dummy if I needed to. It felt good to feel confident this time around.

Since we've come home, Tess hasn't regained her birthweight, so like Lily we have resorted to supplementing her breastfeeds with three formula bottles a day. The first week, we tried just breastmilk with me taking medication, herbals drinks and expressing to get my milk supply up. Like the dummy, this time around I was more than happy to say that I wanted to introduce bottles – bugger anyone who disapproved. Tess has been more settled since she has had the top-up feeds. I just wasn't prepared to let her go hungry like Lily did whilst I fiddled around with my milk supply.

I thought I'd be able to establish a solid routine with her by now, but again I was a bit overzealous. Tess is starting to self-settle, it breaks my heart to let her cry, but sometimes I just have to (like when I have to go to the loo!!).

She's sort of sticking to a three-hourly feeding routine but sometimes she sleeps for five hours or more before she wakes for a feed. The lack of decent sleep is definitely catching up with me. I'm inhaling chocolate and craving coffee and carbs – all to keep me awake, I think, lol.

My mum with the girls

Feelings

While I have been too busy to blog since Tess' birth, I have been itching to write about how I'm feeling.

I have moments of clarity where epiphanies burst through, and then the majority of the time I try to wade through sleepiness, house noise, and the demands of a toddler and newborn to pluck out some sense of what I'm feeling.

Again, I'm having to let go and flow with life. With a newborn, time seeps away, days run into each other and just getting the washing and dishes done makes me feel amazingly organised... even if I am doing it with both my well-worn nipples hanging out of my top (sometimes I forget to put them away between feeds! lol

Days, and in particular the weather, is passing me by. Hot? Cold? Foggy? I'm mainly just seeing it through the window. Not experiencing it makes me feel bizarrely disconnected with the world.

Then I turn and gaze at Tess' face and her eyes connect with mine. Pure love and joy courses through me. She will be my last baby. This time is precious, so to hell with the world. Let it slip by while I fall deeper in love with this perfect soul every day.

I sometimes feel like I am just playing mummies and babies because it is so much fun! But then, maybe that's how it's supposed to feel; mainly joyful, not overwhelming with anxiety like it was with Lily in the early days. So, this is why people have more than two kids, because the first is a shock, the second is joyful and from then you'd know that you can DO this parenting thing. Wow!

I am so glad we've had a second child to experience the difference. At times I feel all zen-like whilst Tess cries the house down; it simply doesn't get to me like it did with Lily. Sure, there are times when enough is enough, but once I pick her up and remind myself that it is simply her way of communicating then I feel peace again.

I think I've grown as a mother since I've had Lil. I try and follow simple principles from my *Buddhism and Motherhood* book – it's my choice as to how I react to my children – feeling anger is a choice and displaying it is definitely a choice I make, not something I can't control. It helps put things into perspective. Lily and Tess don't deserve anything less than love and patience from me.

My ability to be patient and more accepting also helped once Tess was born. I was able to receive visitors better and we even had my in-laws stay with us for five days in Week 2. I'm much less rattled this time around. It made for more relaxed, happy interactions with people who were very pleased for us and who wanted to meet Tess and congratulate us. I suppose it's a sort of state of grace that I am trying to achieve and which I hope I do more often than not.

My sister in law, Sonya and Tess

My Aunty Jill and the girls

Kent's presence home since before Christmas has certainly made the whole situation much, much easier and happier. He is my right-hand man and I hope I am his right-hand woman, too.

Together we've been a great team looking after our girls. He's been mainly concentrating on Lily while I've been caring for Tess. We have a running joke of: How is your girl? Asleep? Happy? Quiet? lol When we have both of them asleep we applaud each other. Yay!!

Not sure how often I'll get to blog these coming weeks. Will try, as the purging of thoughts and feelings is always good for my soul.

Hope life is good your end.

Much love. xxx

Second guessing

I've been second-guessing myself in all sorts of ways.

It manifests in doubt. Doubt in how well I'm caring for Tess; doubt in how well I'm caring for myself... That ol' evil again – huh??!

I sit here, typing with one hand, holding Tess with the other and trying to wolf down a sticky bowl of icecream and topping as quickly as possible – the sugar-rush is intoxicating. My shoulders are burning as if I've been sunburnt, but it's simply the knots in my neck and back twisting up so much they burn.

I'm tired but can't go to bed because Tess hasn't. The ends of my Groundhog days can be tough. Tonight is probably a good night, though. No one is crying, and I have chocolate within my grasp.

Tess is not putting on much weight. Last week we introduced bottles and she made a big boomba leap of 300 or so grams. This week she only put on 50gms. I need to feed her more. I cried today when she was weighed. Yet again I'm in this juggle of feeding breastmilk and formula, trying to maintain my milk supply and her weight gain. It's tricky shit, wrapped in emotions.

I know I'll get past them. Tess will gain weight, I will again begin to lose weight. I won't consume the entire Universe's store of dark, mint chocolate (maybe just half of it – lol), and life will once again seem normal one day, not strangely skewed like it is with a newborn.

I'll keep gazing and smiling at my baby girl(s).

Tess is a month old today, bless her. Lily is smitten with her sister – so cute!

Hiding in newborn land...

You'll find me between breastfeeding, nappies, and rocking (the baby, not myself in a corner just yet). I am in magical, hazy, frustrating and gorgeous newborn land! Add a toddler to the equation and, well... I am lost. I'll pop up now and then and blog (and breathe). Wonder what else has been happening out there in your lands?

My Band GP kindly didn't see the point of weighing me. She said that it is only early days, six weeks since Tess was born, so I shouldn't worry – I'll get back on track soon. Of course, I *am* worrying and that is making me eat a bit more emotionally, often wildly cramming sweet things in to make me feel 'better'!? Old, very familiar and fricking scary behaviour. PLEASE, PLEASE dust-off Keith the Killer for me, Kent, so I can get my expanding arse into gear.

Was thinking tonight that I need to make two things my 'job' apart from raising my gals:

1. to get on Keith as often as possible – just get moving;

2. to make lots of fresh salads, bakes, sandwich fillings, nut dishes etc., that I can grab with one hand out of the fridge and feed myself great, loving food – not shite like white bread and chocolate.

I know the behaviour is due to hormones, sleep-deprivation and emotions. The control factor has a lot to do with it, too. I feel like I have no control, so I am pushing my discomfort down with comfort foods. Oh, I could analyse this 24/7, but right now I am too tired and need to get my boobs out (again) to feed Tess.

I have written on a sticky note and stuck it on my en suite mirror: *Be Kind to Yourself.*

Easier said than done!

I will press on and vent again soon.

Blessings. xxx

Keith the Killer cross trainer

Keith, my friend

Just a mini-milestone to note: I have started exercising on Keith the Killer cross trainer again! I did a 35-min workout yesterday after successfully getting both girls down for a sleep at the same time (yes, I am superwoman at times – lol). I changed into my trackies and sneakers before I put the girls down and had the baby monitor set up in case they woke, then the minute their eyes shut I sprinted up to the shed to work out. It was so exciting!

The CD of music Kent and I put together was awesome and I managed to make it through 35 mins even though there were times when I thought I'd have to stop because I was so puffed. I didn't, though, and surprisingly I felt good – just a little stiff afterwards.

My c-section scar didn't hurt a bit, and today I have pulled up well. In fact, my aim is to get back on Keith today and tomorrow. Looking forward to feeling less wobbles in my butt and beyond now that I'm back exercising! It has been seven months between workouts – eek!

Raw

I feel battered and raw today.

I had to put down our cat, Bruce, yesterday. He had another relapse and his lungs were filling with fluid (due to a bad heart apparently).

It was such a horrible decision to make. I felt oddly grown up having the authority to choose whether an animal lives or dies. The vet said that it was a wise decision because he'd probably get worse and have more episodes, increasing in severity. It was the third time in a few weeks that it occurred. We spent over $1000 on medication and treatment, so we did our best for him. I still feel guilty though. I still feel like I took his life. His brother, Ned, is pining for him. It's very sad.

I can't stop the waves of tears that come over me.

He was in such a bad way yesterday; frothing at the mouth and gasping for air. We tried medication first, but he just got worse. He looked at me with big eyes as if to say, 'help me'. Watching him pass was peaceful, but it now remains in my mind, flicking through randomly.

Ned slept on Lily's legs last night, he's never done that before. His cries through the night for his brother were high-pitched and unrelenting until he finally settled in with Lily. I hope she can give him some of the love he needs.

I know it will get better. I know that it was necessary and that this pain will seem a bit silly to me very soon.

I'm just rolling with it now, though.

Tess was with me at the vet's. I feel like she shared it with me, supported me in a way.

RIP Slinky. We'll miss you. You were a beauty. xxx

Kent and his parents and the kids

Lists

Oh again, it's been a while. Life is passing by quickly up here on the hill, but at the same time not a lot seems to happen.

We've been busy with a week-long visit from Kent's folks and Easter and well, just tending to two kids.

I have an everyday struggle with myself. What can Ailsa achieve today? Four things vie for my time daily, and I have to choose which get left behind:

1. House cleaning/tidying.
2. Exercise/Keith.
3. Sleep.
4. Mind clearing/organising.

Right now, they sort of fall into that order, and if I get the 1-3 things done I feel fantastic. Some days I don't get to any of them, and this is when Ailsa's thoughts become very unkind to her!

Keith must be working his magic again. After starting on him about four weeks ago, I'm keen as to get moving in all sorts of ways. Netball is starting this weekend, and I've been holding my own at training for the last four weeks. I'm even running around the house and doing laps in the shed, all to get my fitness up for the court play.

I have to admit, if I can do anything to make me feel good, it is to get on Keith daily for 35 minutes. It's always a mind struggle – leave stuff undone in the house and move my arse? But I just have to remind myself that afterwards everything seems calmer, not so grim, just all ok. Those endorphins are addictive, I can tell you!

Even though I'm back on track with exercise, the scales haven't been too kind. It's probably been a good thing to have time to get used to my weight-loss before I lose more. I am now familiar with this new body and how it looks. The only thing that is concerning me is that I am not ready for some of the attention my figure is getting. It is so strange that I'm quite uncomfortable with how many comments and looks I got at a wedding the other weekend. I really appreciated how kind people were, but in the end, I felt... well, exposed.

I guess that I'm going to have to get used to that sort of attention again. I remember now, when I was thinner as a teen, how men treated me and, in turn because of the male attention, how other women treated me. Thin wasn't safe then. Thin sometimes doesn't feel safe now. I know that I am a different, confident, wise woman now. I will be safe.

Ok, back to my list, I can hear a two year old chatting to herself. I'm guessing 'have a sleep' therefore won't be something I achieved today... boo!!!

Blessings. xx

Running on empty

I just realised the other day that I am running on empty. I wonder why I don't feel energetic and enthused, even when I wake in the mornings. I am not being refreshed by the small amount of sleep I'm getting, and my body is feeling the effects of the last three months of newborn routine. Blurgh! Oh well, one day soon I'll wake up and realise I am feeling better and more refreshed. It will creep up on me like the exhaustion has. lol

Kent is off interstate for two weeks (or so – eek) work tomorrow. It will enable me to get into routines with the girls and get back to our smaller meals, but it's going to be friggin tough, too. I am shitting myself, just quietly. Time to practice plenty of deep breathing and being kind to myself, and in turn taking good, calm care of the girls.

Wish me luck!!

Mother's Day bliss

On this sunny but cool autumn Mother's Day morning, I am grateful.

The sun is shining through onto my Mother's Day flowers

I've had a hot, milky coffee and have been sung "Happy Mother's Day" (a new version of Happy Birthday Day – lol) by Lily.

I've blissed-out in our rocking chair with a warm, sleepy baby and a snuggly little gal in my lap. I will always treasure my scribbled-on card by Lily, and am grateful for Kent and my mum thinking of me and both calling me this morning.

I am a lucky Mummy.

I love my girls and my life. xx

Alone but not really at all...

I had a burning desire to write to my local friends with young children the other day. This is what poured from my heart and the responses back have been overwhelmingly positive, with most of them saying they, too, feel lonely and isolated but also inspired by each other.

To my gorgeous yummy-mummy gal pals,

I'm writing this between doing dishes and washing whilst both my babies are having a day sleep. I've been wording this note to you all for weeks now in my head and just have to get it down before it enters the ether in my full-up mummy brain.

I just want to let you know that you all inspire me daily. It can be a lonely job being a mum, even when you are surrounded by the noise and chaos of children. I often find myself doing the most mundane household tasks and thinking of each of you at different times. Even though we might not see a great deal of each other, I think about our connection as I drudge through washing bottles, wiping bums, hugging away tears and rocking (myself – just kidding) the girls. We are all doing it – or have done it – and we all have so much to give to each other in the sense of advice, inspiration, or just an understanding ear. This parenting gig didn't come with instructions, try as I might to find them in books etc., most of my knowledge has come from you guys as well as trial and error. I still stuff-up daily, and sometimes I even win a few rounds with the girls and with my own high expectations.

Once simple trips to the supermarket, now tactical game plans, entail getting the appropriate trolley, snacks for the toddler, wipes for any strategic messes the girls throw at me and, of course, two dummies (aka plugs) etc. Sometimes even this simple shopping task seems all a bit too hard and I think of my inspiration. If some of you with three kids or more can do it – then what am I complaining about??

When I think about anything that seems just too damn tough being a mum, I draw strength from you all. We all have our battles and sometimes we just have to wade through them, other times we have to let the current carry us no matter how much we just want to get to the bank and lie the hell down!

I'm not sure when I signed up for part-time solo parenting but somehow, I find myself a bit lonesome up on the hill and I think of you guys maybe feeling the same at times. Whether it's because your boy is working or playing away, working long hours, or just there but not really there... I'm with you. I miss not being able to just get in the car and drive down to the pub for a drink whenever I feel like blowing off steam, and I miss not having work outside of the house to have something else to bloody talk about!

In saying all that, though, I know there is light at the end of the tunnel and I can see that some of you are working/studying/just living lives outside of being a mum. Some are just having drinks with friends a bit more easily these days, and this makes me very happy! You are my hope when I am up to my elbows in the less-than-pleasant joys of motherhood. I will find 'myself' again one day – a new version, but just me.

You might be reading this and thinking 'why would she send this to me? I'm just muddling along being a mum – I don't think I'm an inspiration', but you are wrong. We never give ourselves the credit we deserve. I'd like to give thanks to you for being my friend and for being in my mind and heart when I am putting yet another load of washing on, cleaning the highchair for the twenty-thousandth time, and kissing the scrumptious cheek of a once-crying, now-smiling bubba.

I think this is the toughest but most gorgeous role I've ever had, and I'm glad to be sharing it with you.

Hope this has brightened your day.

Much love always, Ails. xx

P.S. Here's to sharing future chapters of our lives as grandmothers with you guys too. They say that 'children come with labour pains, but grandchildren are pure profit' – sounds good to me! xx

My craft, psych, and conscious consuming

MY CRAFT

I was driving home from swimming this morning and was listening to a musician talk about his inspiration for writing songs when it occurred to me. My blog is my craft. Well, hopefully just one of them, but an important part of who I am. I need to honour my need to journal and document, and to set aside time for it, too. I have a bunch of scratchy notes around the house with ideas to note, so get ready for an onslaught of blog posts – it's been a week of epiphanies again

PSYCH

First, I might catch you up on my psychologist appointment. I actually got something out of it, and I think he may have, too, for future clients. He confirmed that everything I am working through in my head on this weight-loss journey is stuff many people come up against. Losing weight is hard work – physically, but more often, emotionally. The depth of what I am dealing with shouldn't be taken lightly by myself. I am transitioning through lots of 'stuff'. He was pleased that I initially felt the weight-loss was 'too easy' as that is what they are looking for in patients: small, steady losses without dramatically changing their lives = Lap Band success. He also said he understood that being 'too easy' would make me feel uncomfortable after a lifetime of trying to control my weight and that letting go of some of that energy and focus on what I'm eating, weighing etc., is scary.

He spoke of people often not feeling all that bad about themselves at their heaviest weight because in some way it has its benefits: it protects, and it exudes a certain authority. I know that I was using some of my weight to protect myself against unwanted advances from men, also as a buffer from my mother, and probably a rebellion against her constant pressure to lose weight. I've already let go much of that, so I really don't need the protection anymore… some I'm still working through, but I'm getting there. He gave me info about another book he thinks I'll like called *Eat What You Love, Love What You Eat* by Michelle May.

He said she speaks of a pendulum where 'Control' is on one side and 'Out of Control' is on the other. What you are really aiming for is neither, rather being 'In Charge' in the middle and trusting your judgement and being more conscious. I like that! In Charge… yep, that's my new mantra, I think.

He asked me if I'm doing lots of non-hungry eating, and I'm not really. I think I'm eating when I am hungry and not overeating most of the time, but it just doesn't feel very conscious because it's often between feeds/nappy changes etc., so my choices are not quite what I'd choose if I had more time and focus. I do have faith, though, that this phase of baby/toddler caring will pass and I will be more focused soon. It was a relief to note that I'm not really eating emotionally (maybe a bit of TLC choccy and bread), but not like I used to do – almost whole pizzas, yada yada.

He spoke of not getting caught up with numbers on the scale, which I understand, as they usually come back and bite us if we give them power. He liked my goal to get fitter and faster for netball rather than get to a certain weight.

So he gave me some good food for thought, pardon the pun!

CONSCIOUS CONSUMING

I've also realised I've put conscious consuming into practice in a few different areas of my life. The most obvious is eating. I work with Rick Kausman's philosophies that dieting doesn't work, and no food is good or bad. I find when I consciously eat, I crave fresh, flavoursome food (often wet, too, which is interesting – lack of water in my day?). If I am hankering after something else, like a burger or chips, I don't stop myself from eating it but I ask myself what I'm really feeling and if there is anything else that will fulfil the feeling. If no, then away I go and eat it… but often just halting myself will take the desire away.

Along with that, I am also trying to be thrifty and not waste as much food as I used to. Being home on the hill doesn't allow me quick trips to the shops either, so I often eat something that is better for me at home than say a takeaway. I'm mindful of what Lily eats too, so I am loathed to feed her heavily-processed foods.

Apart from food, I am also a more conscious consumer these days. I ask myself if I really need the item I'm considering buying, or if it is just more 'stuff' to clutter our lives. Again, halting the impulse-buy often leads to making do without and hanging onto our money. Win, win!

Just 'waking up' to some of this stuff is mind blowing, and I love seeing the changes in my life.

Other aspects of being conscious have lead me to my next post…

Again… it's just not my stuff!

Back to being conscious again.

Over the last week or so I've had a few conversations with old friends and realised they are caught up in taking on board other people's 'stuff' when they've been drawn into the drama of other people's lives.

I have come a long way; I know it.

Sometimes I feel I am very disengaged compared to how I used to be with people, but then again I was being flung all over the place emotionally in the past worrying about what people thought of me or had done to me when really it was never about me – it was simply *their stuff*. Ahhh, that good old line. I LOVE, LOVE, LOVE you Leonie for teaching me that – mwah, mwah! xx

So these days, I try to not sweat the small stuff or even the big stuff really, because it isn't my place to rescue, worry, or make-right all situations. Sometimes I can help, but by being graceful, kind, and mindful rather than 'doing' anything.

Think this is what world peace is made up of, isn't it?! *Ah ha*

So off I now go to lug some more wood in for the fire.

I laugh when I go from breastfeeding and rocking my gorgeous babe, to stomping around the yard collecting wood and dealing with outside jobs. Goddess power!

Tess had a dawn feed this morning and as the cool morning light seeped into my room, my baby girl's face lit up in generous smiles for her mummy. It was a special mothering moment.

Blessings. xx

Please forgive me

To my gorgeous daughters and husband... please forgive me for this is not the person I want to be.

The yelling banshee Mumma and the whining wifey are not the real me. The real me is trapped under a mountain of mummy responsibilities and can't get out.

Bear with me...

I love you all so much and always.

xxxx

P.S. And hey, from me to you, Ms Ailsa – I love you too. You're doing your best and you know that in your heart.

Take care. x

The five of us together — Chloe came to visit.

MIA

Yes, I've been MIA (missing in action) over the last month in blog land.

July has been pretty monumental for us really.

Kent's daughter, Chloe, came and stayed with us for a weekend and then we all travelled together to spend time with Kent's family.

Chloe was an absolute pleasure to be around. She obviously really enjoyed connecting with her sisters, her dad, and her *gulp* step-mum! lol And we all enjoyed our time with her, too. She was such a help with the kids and just naturally became a part of our daily routines. Really, I could write paragraph after paragraph about the whole experience of getting to know my husband's eldest child, but I think I'll just do what Kent's family is so good at — just letting things be what they are. It was *good*. Chloe is a gorgeous, clever, and kind girl. I feel very, very fond of her. xx

Roughed up

That's how I'm feeling right now — just roughed up.

I wasn't expecting to hear about Kent's new roster: 10 days on, 4 days off... it's kinda killing me, actually. Not sure why. Maybe because I know this will go on for months. I'm kicking myself for getting any hopes up for 8 on, 6 off.

I should know by now to assume the worst and then when it's slightly better it doesn't hurt so damn much. I just feel sorry for Lily, mainly. She's not going to understand. She'll just miss him terribly. Leading up to the next job he's mainly going to be away, bar a week when we are in Qld (thank god for that pre-booked holiday).

So my eyes are scratchy and sore from crying. The sick feeling in my stomach is starting to settle after a night's broken sleep, and this morning I saw a beautiful stream of sunlight through my kitchen window.

So onwards and upwards and two fingers up to the powers trying to pull me down.

Call me stupid…

Call me stupid, but I've just realised that I still have a six-month-old *baby* and a two-and-a-half year old in my care, and it is kinda all-consuming! Especially when the baby has a head cold and can't settle into sleep with her dummy because she can't breathe through her nose. Looks like I have a tough night ahead of me if her sleeps are anything like they've been today. She can sleep in my arms with the dummy being held in her mouth against me, but the minute I put her down she cries then screams… Like now… back soon…

Fingers crossed the steam from Tess' bath may have cleared her out a little. She's sleeping now, and Miss Lily is getting there (chatting away to herself in bed).

I was reading a chat thread today about trying to find some time for yourself, and I have. I've booked some laser hair removal for my legs and bikini line and I've just had an appointment with a plastic surgeon about a breast lift and possibly a tummy tuck too, omg! Big steps to tweaking my body, but steps I've been contemplating for years. So, I'll be less hairy by summertime and then next autumn I'll probably be having the two ops at the same time. Wow!

Now to just remember that even though I want to look like a goddess all the time, sometimes this goddess is just going to have to do with some old trackpants and a top and find herself in a not-so-tidy place (aka my house right now).

All I can say is lesson number one for today: cous cous and kids don't mix

– I'll be finding little bits of the stuff trekked all over this house for months, I'm sure!

Now just breathe, Ailsa – do it for Tess, at least, and of course your yummy-mummy self.

Now off to wrangle the toddler into bed (again).

Blessings! xx

P.S. Remember, Ailsa, *we are all perfect souls in imperfect bodies.*

Lily 2 ½ years and Tess 6 months

Six-month-old baby

Quite a few changes have happened in the last month. I stopped breastfeeding Tess, which broke part of my heart. It was her choice, but it was the final time I'll ever feed one of my babies.

I have just started my first period since having Tess, and it has reminded me in all its glory that that pregnancy/newborn stage is behind me. I'm mourning it a little. I'm working so hard on progressing forward that I feel like I'm not acknowledging what I'm leaving behind.

I will always be a mother now; caring for them in the different stages of the girls' lives. The very newborn days are over – both a blessing and a sorrow. Tess is six months old tomorrow. Kent and I kept telling ourselves that we just need to get through the first year when I was pregnant with her. Well, we are half way through already! Wow.

Numbers, numbers

I've been battling with the scales again. This week, the scales told me I was up. WHAT THE??!! I felt the slimmest I've felt all along, yet the scales were telling me I'd gained. So I promised myself I'd tweak things – get on Keith three times this week and eat smaller meals and stop when I am full (and stop snacking whilst making Lily's meals; I mindlessly put food into my mouth while standing in the kitchen). Then Thursday night when I got my period, the weight gain made sense and in one day I'd dropped down again. Honestly, what does it matter what numbers I see? I am feeling the fittest, sleekest, and happiest I've felt in my body for YEARS… actually, decades! How dare the scales bring me down!

I decided to perch on the scales and manipulate them to show the magic number I seek, with a lot of balancing on the en suite sink and giggling I found it and have locked it into my mind as a picture I can visualise. It really does exist on my scales, and maybe one day I will honestly weigh that little. In the meantime, I'll concentrate on what is GOOD at present.

In general, I just feel like I am rocking outfits I am wearing. I feel like I could run and jump and dance and leap (and often I do) because I feel so light and free and happy in my body.

So take that scales! You can't bring me down.

Oh, and I'm eating brilliantly too. I've also been having delightful handfuls of yummy chocolate. After all, balance in life is everything!!

Our Queensland holiday

Remaining calm

Our trip to Palm Cove in North Queensland was divine.

The weather was gorgeous.

We all got some good Vit D and a bit of a sun-kissed glow.

Lily has blonde streaks in her hair and I have a slight tan – lovely for winter!

Coming home has been a bit odd. Well, actually, I don't think it's sunk in properly yet. I'm sort of vague-ing out, focussing on the small beauties in my day: a leaf glistening silver with a drop of dew, and the smell of warming gum trees in the sun.

I think the calm of the time away has settled into my mind, soul, and bones for a while. I didn't necessarily feel rested (not with two early-birds waking at dawn each morning and needing attention for the rest of the day), but I did feel relaxed.

If only you could bottle this feeling and return to it when times are tough.

I guess I just need to step outside a bit more. That's what I loved about being away – being outside and moving around.

I had epiphany after epiphany, too, while away.

Just stepping off the plane and driving through the cane fields with the wind whipping in through the open window made me realise that I had fulfilled a dream to get back to North Qld, feeling confident and content in my life.

On this trip, I felt I had 'arrived' at a destination in my life I have been so eager to reach – a place of happiness, beauty, grace, and thanks.

Lonesome

I watched a beautiful SA-filmed movie the other night, *The Boys are Back*. One of the lines in the film was this:

"I've got plenty of people to do things *with*, I just don't have someone to do nothing with."

Oh, how true! You can be so lonesome for your love or potential love even when you are surrounded by friends.

I miss you, Kent. I miss us being together and doing nothing... or simply raising our girls and smiling at each other every few minutes as they amaze us.

This is the hard bit about being apart from you.

All my love, always. xxx

Choices

The last couple of days I've found myself in a place in my life where I have made significant changes, but I can't for the life of me see how.

I guess it is so true that 'from little things, big things grow'. Simple choices I've made almost daily for the past few years have brought me to a place where I don't smoke (when in the past I could never see myself quitting), I don't go out boozing every weekend (that was kinda curbed the minute Miss Lily came on the scene – lol!), I have lost weight and I exercise regularly. Wow!!

It gives me hope to make further changes in my life, like getting better at saving and being thriftier – my next challenge!

It goes to show that small, consistent shifts in my day pay off.

A Mother's Prayer

Head space

Quiet

Alone with my thoughts

Still in my body & breath

This is what I crave

Elusive sacred *me* time

To stop & process

To dream & manifest

Please grant me Grace

And Space

The girls in Di-di and Puppa Geoff's garden planting seeds.

Garden fairies

I love that the girls are learning to love gardening through their grandparents. Down here in the hills with my parents and up with Kent's parents, too. They love planting seeds. One day we'll have a beautiful garden for them to play in!

Remember Ailsa

Since I am using my brain today, I thought I'd also jot down a few desires that have been filtering into my heart and mind the last week or so.

I want more time to write, *really* write. Poetry, short stories, blogs, journals.

I am dreaming of escaping for hours outside, in parks, gardens, beaches, cafes and pouring out my thoughts. I just can't be chained to this desk, encumbered by the washing drying around me and the tugging at my leg by a toddler or baby.

I want to delve more into gorgeously-produced filming. I am floored by some of the beauty and sharpness of film and television productions I have recently seen. I want to know more. How do they do it? Could it possibly play a part in my future career? Life? I'm craving capturing beauty through my camera and other medias. I want *art* to have more of a focus in my life.

I want to continue in my quest to get fitter and just move my body more easily. I am even considering a long-term goal to run in a Fun Run, not just walk, but actually push myself and train to run for several kms. I think it will be more likely after I get a bit of extra jiggle removed next year, but it isn't a ridiculous goal... is it?

Along the fitness line, I want to explore other sports... or at least classes in the future. Maybe even a martial arts course for strength and balance. The fitness world *is* my oyster these days. What joy!

Best I stop pondering and check on the munchkins (playing/probably wrestling in Lily's bedroom). I've managed to write this post over the space of seven hours – between my mumma duties and a serious workout on Keith.

Wish I had some time to read all my previous posts because there are a hell of a lot of lessons in them for me to REMEMBER! xx

Perfect

I put a new note on my en suite mirror today: **You are perfect and exactly as you should be today!**

Just got to thinking that the only way to ever feel like I am a.o.k is to remind myself daily that I am exactly where I should be. The Universe has me in the right place/weight/head space that I need to be in every day. No point fighting it and wanting more each day. Surrender and believe.

So... EAT MY SHORTS negative body-image thoughts!! I am perfect just the way I am. And so are YOU, my gorgeous friends.

Love you. xxx

2012

RUNNING / POWER / CHANGE / SASS

It will not make me, nor break me!

These are the words that run through my mind every time I stand on the scales – [this number] **will not make me, nor break me!**

Today I hummed the theme music to *Jaws* (ha ha) as I placed my feet on the metal. It wasn't going to be good after the Christmas break… and it wasn't. I was heavier than my last weigh-in – yikes!!

Oh well, as I have been telling myself during the break: this is not my usual reality. I don't eat/live like this permanently anymore. It's just a blimp (literally – lol) in the landscape.

Kent is going away for work again for a week or so, so that will help get me into a routine with the girls, back eating lightly, and working out on Keith.

I have my running pants now, and will buy myself some light running shoes and then off I'll go.

I'm going to become a runner in 2012!

Farewell, my beautiful Nanna

As I type, the sun is setting on the final day my beautiful Nanna lived on this Earth. She died early tonight after many moons of fading physically and mentally. She and I had some quiet time together last week where we held hands, kissed and hugged, then I took the girls in to see her again two days later. She blew kiss after kiss to us goodbye, and waved happily. What a lovely last memory of her.

I just kissed the cheek of my eldest; her blue eyes pierced me with empathy for my tears. An everlasting memory of Nanna's sky-blue eyes lie in her great grand-daughter's. I was so lucky to have loved you and been loved by you.

In hindsight after losing Nanna

She used to judge me harshly about my weight, but when I saw her the other day she didn't even seem to notice my weight-loss, just simply my face and that I belonged to her – blue eyes, high cheek bones, similar hands etc. What a lot of effort we all waste on body size and numbers when it boils down to love.

I love my family and my friends full stop. I don't care what numbers pop up in your life, I love you all the same. Blessings from a wounded, sad, but ok chick on the hill. xxx

Va-va-voom

Worrying about numbers on the scale is such a waste of time. If I was feeling sprightly enough I'd do a jig, but that can wait until tomorrow. Today I'm trying out the theory that maybe just wearing my 'skins' (running pants) will counter-act the fact that I am cramming whatever I can find into my gob. Surely the chips will be burnt off by my running pants even if I am just reclining on a chair? I believe it, so it shall be so – ha ha.

I was watching an old flick over the weekend – *It Started in Naples* with the gorgeous Sophia Loren. I was astonished by the array of curvaceous women in the film. The male characters were beside themselves over ample legs, hips, and breasts sweeping past them in almost every scene. I was surprised by my own reaction to a dimpled thigh or two – my mind judged them because, compared to the pre-pubescent figures we see on screen these days, they were indeed bigger. It was liberating to see how desirable the curvy women were though, as that is what I will always be.

So onward and upward...

I'm happy to keep a few curves on board. Enough to be va va voom...

Fear factor

Tomorrow it has been one whole year since our baby girl Tess was born.

Tessie's impending birthday is hitting me harder than I expected. Waves of sadness and loss because my last child is no longer a baby. After all the moaning I've done about the early, messy years of Lily and Tess's lives, I am still shocked they are moving so quickly away from being babes in my arms. That also means the life I've known well after three years is now shifting. I may have to go it 'alone' as such in the big, wide world again soon and it's kinda scary.

Tessie has started childcare too, so two of my days are now 'free' (within reason of course!). My heart is torn out when I have had to leave her in tears in the nursery. It's natural, I know. Lily has been visiting her in the nursery section of childcare, which is lovely. She has already taken on the role as her sister's protector and soother. Tess comes home all smiles and giggles so I'm sure she is ok. I just miss them. It's harder when Kent is away, too, as the three of us girls are generally a little team – looking after each other. I know it will get easier and that Tess will learn to love childcare as Lily does. In the meantime, I will take deep breaths and let life *be*.

Funny how the Universe often delivers everything at the one time. I've had a major epiphany over the last month: to study psychology or counselling & psychotherapy at the University of Adelaide. I think I may do it part-time or maybe even full-time if the contact hours agree with family life. It feels that all I have been learning about myself has been leading me here. It is only now, at this age, through my life experiences and my role as a mother that I feel I could offer anyone anything. Watch this space!

Anyway...

Birthday cake cooked – check!

Present sorted – check!

Lips ready for giving hundreds of first birthday kisses to my baby girl – check!

Off to bed I go...

Ciao and blessings. xxxx

Running and baking

I just ran. Well, jogged. But I'm calling it running. It was my second training down at the oval and it was great. I've started with interval training on grass: walk a ¼ of the oval, run a ¼, walk a ¼, run a ½, walk a ¼, run ¾ etc... until I got to run 1¾ laps of the oval.

All in all I was moving for about half an hour and ran/walked seven laps... not bad! I pulled up sore after my first go, but I'm keen to make this a new habit that I love.

Now I've come home and tucked into an amazing tabouli with quinoa, lentils, mint & parsley, and a dollop of homemade pesto. I grew most of the veg and it was yummy!

So how is my healthy lifestyle going? Fab! And how is my healthy self-talk going? Not so fab. Those damn bloody scales are EVIL I tell you, but I feel farking fantastic!!

My skin is glowing, I am getting fitter by the day and my clothes fit perfectly. I think I need to drum up another positive visualisation. I have been thinking about a cake-baking and goal-weight analogy.

It goes something like this...

How often do you open a recipe book and see a gorgeous cake recipe? Yummo, you think! The picture is spectacular and it looks like something you could very well make. You check if you've got the ingredients... well, most of them anyway and then you get into the groove and begin.

First, I choose some good cooking music and make sure I've got the kids out of my hair for a while. I clean up a little, so my work space is user-friendly and then I make a nice cup of tea then go about reading the steps.

I've baked a few cakes in my time, so sometimes I rush ahead and cream the butter and sugar if the first step is to sift the dry ingredients, but that's cool. It still works. Often, I decide to halve the sugar content and I add a few different spices to the mix. I might not have, say almonds, to top the cake, so I go for pistachios or something else I have in the cupboard.

My cake tins are a bit temperamental and can stick, so I often use my trusty loaf tin, and this can sometimes change the cooking time.

I love the experience of cooking, so while I'm going along I feel happy, and sometimes I learn new ways to do things, like sifting the dry ingredients really does help avoid lumps! lol

I have sometimes turned out a few cakes that have a little uncooked spot in the middle, but they've still tasted good and I could cover it with icing. I love lemon in icing, so it usually gets added even if the recipe doesn't call for it.

By the time I get to icing the cake, I often have a bit of a mess on my hands and I'm probably needing something stronger than tea because my patience is starting to run out. I'm also over the idea of eating the final cake because I've been tasting far too much as I've been going along, so could actually be feeling a bit sick at this stage. All in all, though, when I do finally complete the bugger, it looks sort of ok, tastes damn delish and my family can't be any happier to just have cake.

My sense of happiness, simply because I've accomplished it, is awesome too. Yeah, it doesn't look like the picture at all, but it's perfect at that moment in time.

So how does this relate to my weight-loss goal?

I have a goal weight in my mind and how perfect my life will be when I get to it. In reality, I might not get there (aka cook a perfect cake) so that number will be meaningless because it's the experiences I've had along the way that are most important.

First of all, I always add music to my day – dance and workout, it gets me motivated and makes me happy. I also make sure I have my exercise space sorted and accessible all the time. If the kids are around, I use them to get me moving: dancing/bouncing on the trampoline etc.

Sometimes I add different 'ingredients' to my day. Like running or a new fab healthy recipe. Sometimes I fail a bit (like the soggy bit in the middle of the cake), I don't exercise and eat crap, but then it works out in the end. I still manage to pull off an outfit I wouldn't have dreamed of wearing previously. I know, too, that I am achieving the baking of the cake just by doing it. I am achieving my health goal just by moving my body in new ways and eating fresh foods. Even if I do eat a whole bag of chips, I know I will not fall back into old eating patterns permanently. I just dip my toe in the cesspit on occasions, to see why I don't swim there anymore.

I may need a cup of tea or possibly something stronger if things don't go to plan, and often I get a bit messy as I go along but that's just life. It's not controlled and *picture perfect,* it just *is.*

So, I'll get back to my 'baking' and try not to focus on the perfect cake/weight-loss goal picture.

Here's to more runs, great salads and sexy dresses!!

Fat is fascinating

I am sadly addicted to the weight-loss programs on TV at the moment – *The Biggest Loser* and *Excess Baggage*. Of course, I can identify with all the contestants and often end up in tears with them as they progress in their journeys. I am pumped by the workouts they are doing and secretly would love to give some of those challenges a shot… actually, all of them (I know, I'm sick! lol).

I'm really excited to see some of the shifts of thinking about weight-loss on *Excess Baggage* i.e. NOT dieting and not relying solely on the scales as an indication of success. Thank fucking god it is finally being put out there in the mainstream!!

I am so passionate about what they are helping their contestants with – the head stuff that is. It just clicks with me and what I have done/am trying to do. My preoccupation with *The Biggest Loser* then is more like when you just can't help looking at a car crash! That program really is a bloody car crash, but unfortunately the ones being injured are the people there pleading for help. Poor souls. They are being messed up even more in their heads by the weigh-ins and 'nutrition'. No wonder some of them are sneaking food at the camp. I would like to know exactly how many past contestants have gained back their weight and more (no doubt). Shame on *The Biggest Loser* all over the world for selling-out those poor people.

My fitness routine is coming along nicely, and I am so damn keen that on days I don't have a run or Keith session booked, I get itchy feet to get moving. I can't believe it, but I am *loving* my running!!

I ran 5½ laps of the oval yesterday without stopping (plus extra laps walking and running). So I ran at least 2.5kms… fark! My breath and recovery was fantastic, so I know I can do more. Yes, I am slow, but it's not about speed for me, it's about training my mind to push past what I *think* I can't do.

I used to worry about what people would think of me running – was I too flabby, fat, or slow? Now I say in my mind: "FUCK IT, I've had two kids so this is the body I have been left with, and now I am going to use it to its full potential. I don't care what anyone thinks of me running, they can look away if they don't like it". I'm sure people would actually be encouraging me, not insulting me anyway. So that's what I also try to bear in mind.

Cosmetic surgery op date

I will be having my breast lift and tummy tuck on Tuesday the 22nd of May.

Eeek and an *excited shriek*.

Now it's getting real.

I am quietly gazing at my body every now and then and giving thanks for the battle scars and stretch marks that will be wiped off in three-months' time.

I hope I'm making the right decision.

It *feels* right in my heart, and that I trust...

Time flies when you're running around

So it seems I have been blogging in my head because a whole lot of 'stuff' has been going on in my mind over the last month and I swear I have documented it in this blog... but maybe not. Instead, I have been storing it in my mind's-eye blog – the one that I write in my mind while I'm working out.

I have been super switched-on to working out for the past eight weeks. I'm now running 10+ laps of the oval, which equates to 4+kms. I've even had a couple of runs on the road around our place and I'm still *freaking loving it!!*

My mind is now wandering to things I've noticed and been grateful for these last two months. Running outside connects me to nature and beauty. Passing the bowling club on my run the other day, I encountered a beautiful smell and wondered if it was a lady's perfume or a good loo spray – lol. Then I realised it was actually the well-loved and tended rose-garden scent wafting over the fence. I didn't actually stop, but I did smell the roses.

The array of birds – maggies, wagtails, cockies, wrens and other delights swoop around and dance in front on my runs. They keep me company in all sorts of weather. I chat to lots of older local residents on their daily strolls as I run, and I get to see the commitment and work of many volunteers at the oval and various community centres in the area. It's lovely to be able to take note of how beautiful the town is and to remember many happy childhood moments down at the oval and in the community.

I think I have a note buried in a time capsule at the RSL from when I was nine or so. I remember the excitement of walking across the oval to the hall to sing at a Primary School Christmas concert. I remember the donkey that used to live in a nearby paddock, and I remember flying kites with my parents and brother down on the oval. I feel a great amount of pride and connectedness to that space and look forward to my girls also experiencing it.

Running

Warning, bad words ahead!

What the hell is the go with STUFF???!!

It is invading my entire being right now.

I'm overwhelmed by the amount of stuff/crap that is spread across our house/car/shed/yard/life. I swear, all the kids toys, socks, drink bottles, half-eaten packets of things, hair ties etc., come to life in the middle of the night and call out to all the piles of washed, and not-put-away clothes, to have a friggin party!

I cannot see a tidy surface in this FUCKING place.

Yes, it is all generally clean, but not put away because generally there is no farking AWAY.

The distinct lack of storage is doing me in, plus two critters under four that leave havoc in their wake, and one grown boy who doesn't really contribute to the mess, but isn't really up on where any stuff belongs that doesn't live in his shed, so is virtually unaccountable.

So, while I rant and start to twitch as I listen to the library's skipping Shaun the Sheep DVD Lily borrowed today, I feel there may be an underlying issue or two here...

a. I am pre-menstrual (back away now)
b. Kent's about to leave me on Sunday for a week so I'll be solo with the kids (help)
c. I am worried that I'm not financially contributing to the house (stupid super-mum syndrome)
d. There is actually crap all over this house and yet it seemed clean just two days ago (never-ending story)

So what to do, Ailsa?

Put a few things into their hidey holes today.

Get Kent to help me put a few things into their hidey holes tomorrow.

Put the kids into a hidey hole (the shed) for a few hours tomorrow so I can clean one area up before they get to another.

Breathe.

Only accept items containing alcohol into the house between now and the next week, anything else will be deemed stuff and will NOT be accepted.

Breathe again and kiss my husband before he heads off to work.

Cuddle the kids whilst lying amongst the piles of stuff because you cannot fight it forever.

Remember tomorrow will be another day.

Blessings – may your stuff not be getting you down. xxx

Here's to 10 years with my boy xx

Anzac Day 2012. Or shall I say 10 years since I've been with my boy, Kent. xx

Here's a little love letter to him and to the Universe to say thanks for finding him for me...

Many, many moons ago, feeling lonely, a little heartbroken and very negative about past boyfriend choices, I decided to write myself a list of all the attributes I thought important in my perfect partner.

Lo and behold, just a few months later Kent came into my life, kissed me in the rain and even after me playing 'come here, go away, come here, go away', decided to stick with me. At first, the list and he didn't seem to match, but as the years have passed and life has taught me to look at people from all angles, not just my own angle... viola! Kent's wonderful attributes magically match my perfect partner's. Funny how you sometimes get what you wish for.

10 years ago, I was a bit of a messed-up, unhappy person.

I just don't think I would have got to where I am now – being so happy – without the constant support of my love. Kent has been my sounding-board and friend throughout it all.

I can't believe in 10 years we now find ourselves in the middle of the suburban dream (or nightmare, lol), with a solid mortgage, married, with two young kids, and getting to or sitting in middle age – fark, when did that happen to us??!!

Then again, I wouldn't give any of it up to go back to my old life.

Yeah, we're doggy-paddling through some tough years, but we're still swimming. I can even see land in sight!!

I think the changes we have in our lives now that Lil and Tess are here are full-on, but simply gorgeous. The bond we share as parents of our two Earth angels is never-ending. The joy we get from sharing stories and experiences from our girls' daily lives is immeasurable. It is delicious, and we just can't help but talk about them whether they are with us or not.

Getting back to land though, it's funny how you naturally always look to the future and dream of 'better days'. I often dream of just a few years away when the girls will be able to get themselves fed, washed, to school, and off to bed and we can get back to being ourselves a little more. I also dream of the time when Kent and I will be present in each other's presence. Where we will be able to focus more on us as lovers and friends. I long for more long chats over drinks and meals, travelling with my love and letting our hair down together (with less of a hangover and maybe with a run or workout the next day).

I give thanks to Kent for teaching me how to listen, *really* listen, and for teaching me to try and see more than my own viewpoint. Things can be done differently and that is ok.

10 years in a relationship teaches you much. 10 years learning about yourself, making slight changes and still growing with your partner and really LIKING them still is pretty damn great.

I think that might be the key...

I know that I love you, baby, but the icing on the cake is that I really LIKE you (dig you, long for you, miss you, look forward to seeing you, laugh with you and often swoon around you).

Thanks for our first decade as 'Ails & Kent' – can't wait for the next one and then some! Mwah.

Happy Anniversary. x

P.S. We're apart this anniversary, baby, with you working away, but you'll be in my heart and mind on Wednesday – as you are right now. xxx

Kent and I smooching in 2006

Old patterns

I can't stop sobbing.

It's been a while since I've had to solo-parent. Kent is away this week. I'm on my fourth day, and it's relentless. I'm drowning in chewed-up bits of food, toys, dirty clothes, and stuff strewn across the house.

Lily has been particularly pushing my buttons, especially at 4.30am when she decides she's going to wake up and play in her room.

The details aren't the issue here, it's my reactions to them.

I've been yelling, swearing on occasion, and generally getting wild with it all.

The worse thing is that I am mimicking a lot of my mother's behaviour when we were kids, and from my own experience, being on the receiving end is not nice.

Her mood swings from adoring to screaming were simply scary.

Eventually, when I was old enough to get it, it didn't matter how nice she was in between the nasty parts – I didn't trust her, I didn't trust that I was good enough. I instinctively knew that I wasn't. Really crying now. Shit, may have touched on something big here.

I don't ever want to make my girls feel that way but sometimes I find myself caught in a frenzy of anger, like they have wronged me (but of course they haven't, they've just pushed my buttons).

I hope that by simply seeing the patterns of mothering, I will be able to break some of the unhelpful ones.

God, I hope so.

I never want my girls to feel they are not good enough around me.

Still weeping for my little girl inside. She was perfect just the way she was.

Processing...

It's got to be about CONTROL – the whole sordid scenario between my mother and me.

I am desperately trying not to let her push my buttons, I am desperately trying to keep it all in perspective. That it is *her* stuff and *my* stuff – not necessarily about *us* at all.

She compared me with her loathed mother-in-law today (very below the belt). Actually, she threw every nasty doozie at me today and I did my best to deflect them. She was looking for a fight, a good old-fashioned screaming match. I'm seething, but I didn't bite (much).

I told her that I wasn't taking any of it on board and that they were her issues she needed to sort out.

She even told me to use my running time to really think about how much they (my parents) do for me (caring for the girls) instead of criticising them. That really pissed me off. How dare she impose herself on my own special time while I run (because of course now I *am* going to think about her – arghh... maybe I'll just give her one minute of thought then cut her off!!).

I can see that she feels criticised by me, but anyone who tries to mess with her control is deemed critical or manipulative (well that's the pot calling the kettle black!! ha).

Listen to me, tied up with her crap. Damn it, I should know better.

Sorry for the boring blah blah blah fucking families post.

At least I'm not sobbing today (yet).

Off to wrangle the kidlets...

Come home, Kent! Please.

Mindfully gorging myself

Good golly, I have been doing a bit of crazy eating this last week.

I have had several days where my appetite is minimal until late afternoon, so I've got by on a couple of coffees and picking at the kids' food without thinking about a meal for myself. Then the evening comes around and I want to soothe myself into a comfy haze with masses of food. Sometimes to the point of feeling uncomfortably full, and that is rare for me these days as I have to put in a long, concerted effort to eat that much.

I know what is happening. I am conscious of pushing down some pretty uncomfortable feelings with food. There you go, that word just came up again – uncomfortable. That must be it.

Of course, I am approaching the operation in two weeks, which is super exciting and super frightening. It makes sense I'm feeling a bit out of sorts. A lot is going on in my head: what will I become? Will I be able to handle a more 'perfect' body? Where the hell am I disappearing to? Because I can see myself shrinking in the mirror and it still shocks me.

It makes sense that old patterns pop up where I am eating to almost conserve my old self.

Thankfully, my running and workouts are semi-containing the almost binging behaviour.

I have also been getting lulled into *The Biggest Loser* dieting industry mindset that *maybe* I need to diet as well as exercise, and then I sit up and slap myself because I KNOW BETTER!

I'm just asking myself: am I eating mindfully? I guess I am, but when does the gorging stop? That's all I want, just to eat lightly until I am satisfied. Maybe my satisfaction has to come from somewhere besides food.

What do you think?

Blessings. xxx

A week until my tummy-tuck and breast-lift op

Thought I'd make the title very clear to look back on in the future.

OMG are the words. This time next week I will have new sitty-up boobs and a different shaped tummy. Biiiiizarre...

This feels like a dream, because it is what I have always wished for (especially the breast op as I have never been comfortable with my breasts from the moment they grew... and then hung).

It is so empowering, but so much 'about me' that I'm feeling a bit guilty about the focus I'm putting on myself and my appearance.

I have begun my hospital list already and will begin to pack my bag.

To quote Rosco, my beloved father-in-law: It's all go at the show!!

lol xxx

My father in law, Ross and cheeky Lil

Two sleeps...

Two sleeps until my operations.

The house is organised and almost spick and span.

My bag is semi-packed.

My awesome mother-in-law, June, arrives tomorrow.

I have a glass of sparkling in my hand.

Think I'm ready...

Kinda looking forward to the 'down' time.

Just one more big run tomorrow before I pop the running shoes away for a few weeks.

Feeling pretty excited and pumped!

xx

I am a brave, bold woman

I am a brave bold woman
I am such a brave bold woman
Walking right into the dragon's mouth alone

I am a brave woman
I am such a brave, bold woman
Seeking love and beauty, I go on my own
I go on my own

Seeking love and beauty on my quest I go
And no matter what may happen
I know I will grow.

(The Gaia Choir)

Thanks to my mid-wife Marijke for introducing me to this song.

This bold woman is walking into the dragon's mouth tomorrow. Not necessarily alone, as I know I am supported with buckets of love and well-wishes from my family and friends. I also know my grandmothers' spirits will be with me. Ultimately, I will be entering the theatre on my own and walking into the dragon's mouth… the love for myself and beauty I seek will be mine, I am sure.

So off I go to bed, to rest a few hours.

Tonight, I farewell my beautiful saggy skin full of history of pregnancies and a bigger self.

Tomorrow I welcome my new body parts. I will saviour their beauty and give thanks for new-found confidence.

Thanks for walking with me on this journey.

Blessings and Love. xxxx

P.S. I kissed my running shoes goodbye for a few weeks – I will miss them! LOL!!

I'm home post-op

So I'm home... healing and functioning to a certain degree. Physically, I have changed, and boy have there been some emotional changes too.

I have needed to be a bold, brave woman.

DAY 1

After four hours on the table and then time in recovery, I got back to my room – foggy and basically immobile. The surgeon was happy with the surgery.

I tried to sit up on the edge of the bed after having a cup of tea and either the movement or the tea (or both) had me reeling with nausea. I was given an anti-nausea drug and immediately had a massive panic attack.

I felt trapped by my immobility, the constant pain, and I felt hot and cold. I was completely freaking out just wanting to run out of the room, but I knew I couldn't. The only thing I could do was sing to myself in my head *"I am a brave woman. I am such a brave, bold woman"*, and repeat over and over: "This too shall pass".

I breathed as deeply as I could, thought of all the people who have had it worse in hospital beds. I drew strength from them all and I gave thanks for my circumstances. Then I took more pain relief and slept off and on. Each time I woke and the panic rose, I gave thanks and breathed it away.

DAY 2

I was beside myself with happiness for getting through the panic, though I was still nervous that it would return (it didn't, thankfully).

I tried to sit up again but nearly passed out, so back onto the bed I went.

That night the surgeon came and asked the nurses to get my blood taken the next morning to check my iron levels. My blood pressure was down, and they were confused by my dizziness. I was healing well though.

DAY 3

I tried to sit in a seat next to the bed, but I was as white as the walls and again thought I'd faint. My haemoglobin levels were severely low. I needed a blood transfusion – WTF?? More anxiety, but also relief they picked it up without sending me home anaemic and lethargic.

DAY 4

I was given a shower and I got to wash my hair and see what was under the bandages. OMG... not bad, I thought! I had several units of blood during the day and slowly started to feel a bit better.

DAY 5

I left the hospital and came home to my babies, which was lovely.

So now I'm in a bit of la la land – fuzzy-headed, the days are blending into each other and I am trying to let control go of the house/the children's care etc., but it is soooooo hard! Family have been doing a brilliant job, of course, and I need to back off, but it's not in my nature to lose control.

I did note a few things in the hospital about what I have learnt this week:

I am so *grateful* for my life, my body, and the care I was given in hospital (it was wonderful).

I was inspired by other people's stories of resilience – they got me through the panic and pain.

I'm sure I felt the flutterings and shadows of loved ones' spirits as I drifted in and out of sleep. They were fussing around me, caring for me. xx

I am so thankful for the unconditional love I received from my family and friends through this very personal choice and experience. Everyone has been extremely supportive.

I am a brave, bold woman.

The pain and discomfort will pass.

I have a lot to process as my body moves through these changes.

My work here is not done by any means – emotionally or physically!

I'm munging into yet another salad sandwich with cheese. Seems a bit of a body craving. I'm going with it, because one thing I DO know – my body is a very clever thing!

Much love & light to you all.

Blessings, Ailsa (version 2012). xxxx

Struggletown

I've been home for over five days now and even though I'm sure I've made small amounts of progress every day, I still feel like I've been hit by a truck.

The toughest part is the swelling.

Sleeping at night is when I get more anxious. I have to lie on my back with a pillow under my knees, and sometimes I get pain down my back that I can't stop unless I get up. I feel trapped again, just as I did when I had my panic attack.

After I shower, I have to dry all the dressings with a hairdryer, the effort is almost beyond me.

Shadows/reflections

I caught a glimpse of my reflection in the kitchen window today. Half obscured by shadow and splintered by dirty rain marks on the glass, my worn face looked back at me. My hair is oily; I haven't showered today or left the house. My dressings are reacting to being wet, and are hurting and itching me beyond belief after showering. My lip is splitting on one side, my eyes look tired and more lined. I feel like a shadow of my former fighting-fit self – the sick, broken version.

Kent left today for five days work interstate. He's been my rock. I'm scared without him here if things go wrong, say, in the middle of the night. His folks are here for two more nights.

Please let me find some strength and let my body heal well and quickly.

I'm frightening myself with the knowledge of what I've done to myself and the responsibilities I have to two very young children in my care.

This too shall pass… I know. xx

48 hours later…

Sorry for my last miserable post. It's where I was, but I'm in a much better frame of mind now. My muscles feel stronger every day and my wounds are healing. I have new, very minimal dressings on now, which has brought on other concerns – my god, I feel like Frankenstein's monster, with stitches around my nipples and the giant shark bite across my tummy. Looking at myself last night made me a bit queasy as I tried to come to terms with the gruesome aspects of being sliced and stitched – blurgh. Can't wait until I have a little less puckered, stitched-up skin to look at.

Healing vibes, and don't-look-at-yourself-in-the-negative vibes are needed here please!

I've probably gained weight sitting around eating comfort food cooked in my new Thermomix machine (which is AWESOME).

I can feel my misery-hunger building as the day goes on and remember that most recently if I felt as crap as this, I'd exercise. I am missing Keith and running sooo much. I actually feel very disconnected from my world right now, as getting out in the fresh air and running really helped to ground me and make me feel more present in my day and within my surrounds.

Interesting stuff.

'Normality' is creeping back into my life

This last week has been good. Normality has been creeping back into my days. I've been getting back into a routine with the kids.

Still wish I could have a holiday from myself (well, my body), but it's getting better I guess.

Tomorrow is five weeks post-operation.

I did my first Keith workout (with the tummy binder on) this morning – yay!

Hot and not so hot

Week 8 post-op has been a bit of a roller-coaster ride.

The not-so-hot part is that Kent is flying out for possibly two weeks tomorrow. My heart always breaks for me, but especially the girls when I know he's about to go away.

I'm also about to hit six weeks where my folks will be away. I hate this time of year when this always seems to happen; it's freezing cold and everyone pisses off on me and I'm left with all the responsibility. Whinge over – lol.

The hot part? I have begun to run again, for real! Whoop, whoop!! I ran 3km on Wednesday around the Uraidla oval and felt great. This morning I've run 4kms from home, including up the big-arse hill leading back home.

It was just lovely to be out in the fresh air, feeling the sun on my skin and smelling the earth. I could hear all sorts of bird calls and chatter of people and animals in the valley. I love feeling connected to my little local patch of the world again.

My body felt ok too; not as fast or as confident, but it remembered what to do and my breath wasn't too strained. I'm back on track, thank goodness, after eight weeks on the sidelines.

Running inspiration

I got out in the glorious sunshine today for a 5km run. I did a local loop and hardly saw a soul, which was lovely. I concentrated on the noises I heard along the way – babbling brooks, little creeks tinkling down grassy hills, kookaburras, black birds and many other birdies chattering. I heard some scuttling in the bush along the road, something smaller checking me out as I passed by. I can't tell you how beautiful it was. I am always overjoyed to be amongst nature when I run.

Chocolate factory win

So even though life has been a bit shitty and I've gained weight since the op, I still had a fantastic win the other day.

It was Father's Day, and we decided to take a day trip with friends. It was a glorious spring day and our spirits were high as we became tourists in our local area. Kent mapped our route and we started at a cafe for coffee, then headed to a chocolate factory, cheese store, winery, brewery and then home to ours for a bbq.

In the past, whilst trying to lose weight, I would have felt a huge level of anxiety about going to all of these tempting places – how can I stop myself over-indulging? I would have felt like I was the biggest in the group, and in the venues. I still was, but not like I have been in the past. This day I stopped and smelled the roses. Enjoyed each venue and tried what others did. We did buy sweets, chocolate, cheese and wine, and it was ok. I didn't feel scared of the experience like I have in the past. I could be a normal person and eat a sweet... or not. The chocolate factory especially didn't worry me as I could have it all if I really wanted... but did I really want it? Ah, no... Maybe a choc bullet or five, but not every bag there.

It was an epic moment for me.

I wasn't ruled or owned by food.

Another win and a bloody beautiful day to boot!

My jewels

Oh how I love my girls! Lil and Tess are my ultimate inspiration and the jewels in my life.

They sleep in the same room now and have become really close. Tess is now saying "Lily, Lily, Lily". In summer they'll be two and four. Wow!

Girls blowing kisses

My big girl Lil

Blessings and happy times xxx

Oh, and btw, it's been four months since my op. How little time has passed really, but it feels like forever ago. Helps put into perspective that I am only now really healed (and may still be healing internally), so I need to again, as usual, cut myself some slack!

I'm doing good. Pat on the back Ailsa J Robson, pat on the back! lol xxx

Shellshocked

I am not quite sure why I am feeling so affected by the Jill Meagher case but after today's news that she was indeed abducted, raped, and murdered, I'm actually feeling it in my body: pain, sorrow, shock and nausea.

Of course, I know I am identifying with it personally – as a young woman who has walked alone at night under the influence of alcohol. I am also a wife to a beautiful man who has been waiting at home for me while I've been out having a few drinks. I also call my brother on occasions when a bit drunk, because sometimes I just need to connect with him.

Looking at my girls, I ache thinking of their futures and having to let them go to experience the world – the horrid parts as well as the magical.

I do know that what will be, will be. Horrific things happen to good people. It still hasn't stopped my tears, though.

I am just sending all my love and light to Jill and her family. I'm sure she'd be amazed by the powerful, common voice amongst women and menfolk saying this is just not right!

Look after yourselves and look after each other in this world of unknowns.

Blessings to all... and love always.

Love is the only way. xxoo

Juggling

I wrote myself a note Saturday night after wine and homemade pizza – *Why Can't You Workout Every Day? Just try!* xx

So yesterday I put Tess down for a sleep and took Miss Lil up to the shed with me so I could bust a move on Keith. Three interruptions (including replacing Tess' dummy mid-workout), and about an hour later I was in a pool of sweat. It was a tough workout because I didn't quite realise how much focus you need to keep going. My head was all over the shop, watching and talking to Lily and listening for Tess over the monitor. My energy was being sapped before I had even started to sweat!

Anyway, today I ran the farthest I've ever run – 7.5kms and one third of that was uphill (big, big hills). I feel a bit bloody awesome! Tomorrow I'll hit Keith again with Miss L in the shed with me. Fingers crossed it all pans out.

xxoo

Funrun photo with kids

Farkin funrun

So far, so good. Four days into my daily workout experiment. It can be done!

Oh, and on Sunday I've entered a 5km FUNRUN!! What the?! Run and fun together... surely not?

I will tell you if it is fun after I get over my phobia of running in groups (I was always at the back of the pack in the past at school sports, if not the last person. I have demons to deal with obviously).

***OMG... Funrun report!

Well it wasn't awfully fun, or too challenging except for my self-doubting thoughts.

I did it, and I might even do one again. 10km next time, and then one day a half-marathon – 21 kms! Eeek!

I felt pretty bloody awesome for a few days until I received this email about my results...

Provisional RESULTS for Hardy's McLaren Vale Half Marathon events 2012.

AILSA ROBSON – Entrant 8022.

Congratulations on completing the 5.00 km run.

Your position overall was 106, placing 12 out of 13 in your Female 35-39 age group.

From the South Australian Road Runners Club.

... so, yay to *second to last!!*

Kent said he was still proud of me, so that was nice.

I wasn't there to race anyone anyway, just to beat down the voice in my head that said I couldn't do it. So, pftttt shitty voice, I did it!!

Onwards and upwards. xo

What the F*#@???

I hadn't heard back from Adelaide Uni re my Masters application so I emailed the admin person from Counselling & Psychotherapy and this is the reply I received:

Hi Ailsa,

I'm surprised you haven't received a letter from SATAC by now. I'm sorry to inform you that you were not successful in gaining a place in the program.

Best wishes as you continue decision-making regarding your future, we wish you every success in your endeavours.

Kind regards

So after I got my breath back and stopped a gut-wrenching sob, I thought... *I'm not done* and rang the co-ordinator of the program with whom I'd spoken with on a number of occasions. She was as surprised as I was that I wasn't successful in the interview. I wondered if it was because I had applied for a Masters straight up and wasn't up to that level, but no. Apparently it was on the three aspects in the interview: potential counselling skills such as active listening, a sense of drive and enthusiasm, and the ability to work on self-discovery.

How did I not pass those things in the interview?

I said I was floored by the outcome, and could I possibly be interviewed again. Or, do I have to apply again next year? She said the university has a mandate to give a second chance (but they've never been asked before) and she'd look into me having another interview after reviewing my interview notes.

She said she can't promise me an interview, but I will know within the next two weeks as interviews are being held late November/early December.

So... WHAT THE FUCK??? I ask myself now.

One thing I know, I'm not ready to let it go yet.

If I don't get in, where on Earth does that leave me in 2013? Just a damned housewife, and that won't cut it. I need MORE. (I type this as Tess is crying at the baby gate trying to get to me.)

Let's see what comes of it all now. Fingers crossed it all pans out otherwise I may just lose it trying to work out what to do with my life if I don't get back into study!

I am a water baby at heart and I love the surf

I also adore my baby brother, Nick x

Beach holiday

So we had a family beach holiday that was great. A little tough being under the same roof as my mum for five nights, but we didn't kill each other. I spent every day running/walking/swimming. We all got some exercise in one way or another as we left the cars behind most of the time. My bro came down too, which was cool. It was nice to be all together, and that's what was important.

I had epiphany after epiphany as I always seem to do around the ocean.

The first day I ran I realised that I was running past these rocks where I sat many years ago in despair over my life (living off my parents, studying but not feeling connected to anything, no love, lonely and overweight). At that time I wrote a poem about those massive rocks with imperfections, looking much like my ample thighs and droopy breasts and wondering why they were still loved by the ocean, caressed by the waves.

If only that girl could see her future womanly self, running past her and feeling fit, happy and loved even with imperfections. That girl thought she was a goner; she'd never be smaller, especially since she still had babies ahead of her (hopefully). She never imagined herself as a mother of two gorgeous girls, living comfortably with her beautiful husband and being educated, capable, and certainly much, much more healthy physically and emotionally.

I told my dad, he was really moved by it. I am one lucky woman and lucky to know it too!

Six months post-op! Where did that time go?

OMG on Thursday it will be six months since I had my op.

I am sitting here, after a 6.5km run in a bikini top (which has become my warm weather uniform already) and shorts. I have a semi-tan and I was confident enough to wear the bikini top and shorts down at the beach last week (a family beach mind, with lots of other mummies & daddies with droopy body bits). Life is incredible!

So, all in all, at the six-month mark, I would say the surgery was a SUCCESS!

I am certainly not perfect, but I remember what the wise midwife at the hospital said when I had Tess (who'd had surgery herself): I'd never be

100% happy with the final result, as nobody is 100% happy with their bodies. I can work with this, though, and I am.

Blessings & Love.

xoxoxox

Speak the fuck up – always!

I left a phone message for the uni coordinator I've been speaking with today requesting any news on my second interview.

She called back and said I would be granted a second interview. She said the only thing that stopped my success in the first interview was that the interviewer didn't get a clear understanding of why I really wanted to do this course.

I said I could possibly see why that could have been the case because I don't have a clear picture of the outcome of this study, but I am very willing to see where it will lead me, and I am strongly looking forward to the learning. She said that was very valid and I didn't need to change myself. I said, I don't think I could at this stage anyway and thanked her for the follow-up and that was that.

Well, bugger me. Seems if you don't have your future career mapped out in fine detail, you don't get a shot at this course!

In all fairness though, I was a bit tongue-tied and may have seemed ambivalent regarding where I wanted to go in my career, because frankly, I don't know what I want to do with this qualification! I'm just coming back into the real world from the haze of mothering two young children.

As Kent said, lucky I didn't simply accept that I was unsuccessful as many others would. If I do get in, best I flog them with HDs all round – ha!

Now enough cockiness, as I don't want to jinx myself.

I'm just grateful for this second chance, but I think I may be super nervous during the second interview. It's coming up in the next couple of weeks. Fingers crossed!! xo

My scales suck

Can I do this for the next five weeks? Scrutinize myself with the scales and survive?

Today the fuckers said .8kg gain, but then my 'fat content' went down 2%, so is it new muscle or what?

Quite frankly, I don't trust my scales whatsoever as they can change their mind between .5 to .8kg with just a wiggle on the en suite floor to another spot (which of course I do until I get the lowest weight – lol).

This is further evidence that weighing myself regularly just doesn't work for me. Leading up to my Friday am weigh-in, I started to freak and even had cereal for dinner last night (partly because I was dead tired after cleaning, but also partly because it helped me to lose weight when that's all I could eat at night whilst pregnant). I've exercised and eaten well and lightly this past week, so all should be well. Why then have I started second-guessing, starving, and berating myself when in fact I feel friggin awesome this week? Slender(ish), fit and beautiful. Surely this was my aim all along, not a number on a scale!

I have also realised my scales may be possessed with 'bad energy' – lol. My parents (not very kindly) gave me the scales as a 'gift' about 15 years ago, and they have been with me through thick, thicker, and then slightly thinner. Maybe I need a brand new spanker with good weight-loss energy that also gives me lots of positive messages: "Hi gorgeous... stuff this number, you look damn HOT! Plus, you have a fine, wicked mind!" Ba ha ha!!

Dumb arse scales/celebrating with the queen/10km run post!

So, I have ordered a brand new, spanker set of scales and they'll be arriving soon – yay!

In the meantime, I 'had' to use my old psycho scales and guess what? A loss of .6kg with a gain of 3% in fat content – *supposedly!* What the??

I'll take it anyway, especially after the week of indulging I had (and am still having, as she sits waiting for her pizza to cook, mmm).

The 'queen' (aka Kent), arrived home and I promptly started eating 'man' serves for meals again with him and drinking like a fish. It was fun though; we had such a lovely week of small family outings, meals out, shopping excursions together and bbqs and movie nights at home. I lurve that boy so much! xo

So even amongst all the celebrating, I managed to tick off a HUGE 2012 goal this week. I ran 10kms straight! It was a 35°C day and even though I ran in the morning, it was still damn hot! I am super stoked as I probably still had more in the tank and I recovered without any issues, almost like it was any old run. I guess it was only 2.5km more than my longest run, but in my mind, it was a marathon. It goes to show that yet again, my body is stronger than my mind gives it credit. I could actually do a half-marathon one day and I probably wouldn't die! Je-sus!! lol

So what next? Do a few more 10km runs when I get a chance on cooler days. I keep needing to remind myself how far I have come from simply running a ¼ of the oval then walking a ¼ etc., in January of this year. Amazing.

So, I have been feeling incredibly good even though the scales have been dodgy, and I am now eating with my usual pre-menstrual passion, ha! I have felt slender, fit, tanned, and sexy. My 'winner, winner chicken dinner' online clothes purchases have helped too.

Not a fluke

Seems being able to run 10kms straight was not a fluke. I just did it again. Woot, woot!!

Here's a beautiful quote that really spoke to me today:

"I always loved running… it was something you could do by yourself, and under your own power. You could go in any direction, fast or slow as you wanted, fighting the wind if you felt like it, seeking out new sights just on the strength of your feet and the courage of your lungs."

- Jesse Owens

Blessings my friends. xoxox

I'm in! To Uni that is!

I've been offered a place in the University of Adelaide's Counselling & Psychotherapy program after my second interview today was successful.

Woot, woot!!

I'm really not sure what happened in the first interview as today's was very similar. In fact I was more tongue tied because I was nervous I wouldn't be successful again... and then I get in! Very odd. I honestly think they lost or muddled up my application rather than me not 'passing' it.

Anyway, water under the bridge. I am now in and already shitting myself about how I'm going to fit any study into my life.

I will simply try to breathe and let it all play out.

Lily as a carrot

Our little carrot

Beware, Mumma bragging about to begin...

Our beautiful big girl Lily had her first ever ballet concert the other weekend and she was, of all things, a carrot in Beatrix Potter's, *Peter Rabbit*. *cute*

She loved being on stage and was so happy about the whole thing. She was apparently brave and happy by herself with her class backstage. I'm very proud as I think being able to stand in front of a crowd and feel confident is an amazing gift to have.

I just wasn't expecting to need a box of tissues to watch the performance. I was blubbering before she even got on stage at all the gorgeous little kids in their sweet costumes: butterflies, robin red breasts, kittens, bunnies, etc.

What a new-found joy for me, watching my baby do well in her own right separate to anything I've taught her. I'm one proud Mumma!

No weigh-in this week

So I forgot to weigh in this morning. Why? Because hippos don't weigh themselves – lol. This hippo just ate bacon, an egg, smoked salmon, Turkish bread and cold turkey for dinner (oh, and cucumber to make it healthy). I haven't worked out either. I will not be surprised if I wake up tomorrow and be 1000kg again. Eeek! Hungry, hungry hippo – look out!

Oh well, it is holidays after all.

2013

UNI / ACCEPTANCE / HIGHS / LOWS

The Universe is saying...

The Universe is saying... not to worry about the scales!

I jumped on Friday am on the flattest surface we have in our house and weighed myself. Yep, about 2kg up... then I did it again – same spot, no wriggling and they were up about 4kg.

I love my new set of scales but seriously? What the...?

How am I supposed to take my weigh-ins seriously?

I guess I'm not supposed to. I guess the true indicator is how my clothes fit, and how I feel (fit, puffy, lean, lazy?).

Right now, I'm feeling the post-Christmas/New Year haze and bloat but I know I'll get back on track.

We had River Day on Sunday, took up the boat and I had a go on Kent's tube, which requires a bit of hanging on! Well, I certainly noticed my fitness level is WAY up compared to this time last year. My body felt completely different – lean and strong, and yet my weight is probably not much different than last year.

Very, very interesting...

Bit sad that Kent is leaving to go back to work on Thursday.

We'll just have to get into the swing of it all again and include uni and Lily at kindy into the equation too. Eek!

2013 is going to be a year of changes.

Ciao & blessings. xoxoxo

Kent freaking me out going backwards on the tube

Going, going, gone...

The heartache has kicked in already.

Kent is leaving again tomorrow for work away after being home for three weeks.

He'll be home in a week, but right this minute it feels like he's leaving us for good. It always feels like that. My heart is in my throat, especially when I think about how the girls will be tomorrow – so, so sad.

He begins the process of gearing up for work the afternoon before he leaves.

He packs his things, sorts out stuff that can't wait a week, and mentally switches into work, so therefore switches off from us.

He'll leave the house before we're awake in the morning.

Hence the going, going, gone...

Sometimes I simply hate this part of our lives; having to be separated 50% of the time.

We'll cope, we always do, but I wonder if that bit of our hearts that gets chipped away each time he leaves is doing us all damage.

Only hindsight will tell.

Bye, bye, baby. xx

Update

Hi there!

I have been thinking about things to blog about daily and then life has got in the way of reporting! Go figure!

I can safely say that my anxiety levels leading up to the start of uni are through the roof, so I have been 'medicating' myself with running, bubbles, minimal sleep, tv cooking shows, and general fussing around the house and kids. All in all, I'm neither relaxed, nor organised. I'm in a bit of a flap, I suppose you could say.

I tentatively picked up my first text book last night and slowly opened the cover imagining a monster of big words to eat me up, and low and behold I liked what I read! I even underlined parts that spoke to me and ticked philosophies that mimicked my own. Maybe I can bloody well do this?! Ha!

Let's hope my lecturers are as interesting as the author.

So, let's get some musings down then...

BODY

I'm almost nine months post-op and am feeling finally quite lean and taut. Sure, I don't have a rock hard six-pack, but I am feeling stronger in my core. I have been continuing my interval training on Keith for over a month now and it may have helped me to lose fat and tone up more. It certainly has helped my ability to recover quickly after running up big hills. I'm smashing 8.5km runs with ease and wanting to go farther if it weren't for time constraints and hot weather.

I had the best run of my life recently on a cool day with light rain. It was so peaceful and the smell of the rain on the earth and foliage around me were intoxicating. I am so lucky to be able to run in the picturesque Adelaide Hills. People have asked if I've lost weight, and Kent has said I look and feel firmer (the best compliment ever!). The 'stoopid scales' are still lying to me, saying I haven't lost, but I won't let them make nor break me.

The proof is in the pudding (or less pudding, I guess, ha!).

BABIES

OMG, my babies are really growing up. Lily started kindy this term and is super happy (which I'm delighted about and sad about as she moves further away from being my baby girl). Tess has moved from the nursery at childcare into the toddler room and is now two – bless her little cotton socks.

These girls are rocking my world. It feels like we've been apart from Kent a lot recently, but maybe it's because I've been pretty disconnected to him even when he's home. I've been getting out a bit socially, which has been awesome but then I don't feel as grounded as I do when I'm home and 'sorted'. Anyway, he's back in two sleeps, so we'll get some one-on-one time again, hopefully. One night, the last time he was home, he was brilliant whilst chatting to me about my fear of uni. His support and care means so much to me.

I am very lucky to have such an understanding, wise, sounding-board and friend. xx

Not dieting but feel like I am :(

I have been feeling fit, pretty trim, bronzed, and generally healthy and happy.

This week I saw my Band GP. Anyway, we discussed my weight and this time she said she'd like to see her patients get down to a BMI of 27-28 as it is still a very healthy BMI and the 'ideal' BMI of 25 might push some people's weight down a little too much (including mine). So my BMI is around 31-32 – I have some work to do!

I came away with grand plans of losing .5 to 1kg per week, but as we all know that would probably mean *dieting* and she strongly said not to get into that mentality because I may well lose the weight then bounce back up.

I liked the suggestions she gave (except weighing myself) as I feel I've not been awfully good at listening to my true hunger and satiety signals. Simply put, I know I can tweak things and hopefully those tweaks will make a huge difference.

So now I'm here, three days after my appointment and I feel like I am dieting.

I guess it's the constant thought-process that is killing me. I don't *want* to think about food 24/7, but I am… and not in a positive way like '*mmmmm looking forward to those Fri night chips with wine and homemade pizza*'.

My brain is saying: *Who cares if it's Friday? You are committed to losing weight, forget the chips, cut the wine down and that pizza isn't a great idea.*

How about tuna, salad, and water?

Of course, my brain then screams back: *I CAN'T DO THIS!! I LOVE FOOD. FUCK THIS!!*

I have to say I'm in a combo of pre-menstrual hormones, ongoing pain from a sinus infection, Kent isn't home, I'm stuck here alone with the noisy kids, I'm tired and I'm stressed about things, including uni starting next week. Great timing to 'not diet', Ailsa. Er der.

Anyway, I'm sure my positivity will come flooding back next week when I'm looking forward to Kent's return. The uni orientation day will be over, and I'll get a few workouts in for my mental and physical health.

So how do I get my brain sorted?

TRUST, Ailsa, TRUST!

What do I really feel like eating?

Actually, my body *is* wanting tuna, salad, and water... and maybe a little chocolate. It's just my emotions that are screaming out they aren't being satisfied.

I have asked myself what would make me immediately happy right now, and it's not a whole lot of food. Number one is sleep, and then to get out in public without the kids and possibly go for a big, long walk in the fresh air (simple huh?).

Don't get me wrong, I'm not denying myself anything. I will eat whatever I really feel like, but as I ask myself the question, maybe it needs to be bigger than 'what do you feel like eating?' Maybe rather it's 'what would make you happy right now?' *Then* I may be able to shake this feeling of dieting doom.

I think I'm just a bit miserable.

Blessings, guys. Hope your weekend is rocking! xoxoxo

Kent and I – loved up

Seven-year itch

Happy seven-year wedding anniversary to my love, Kent.

The only itch I want to scratch is the itch to travel with you, baby, and to experience more of the world with you, my friend.

Loving you more each year as we get to evolve together as individuals and as a couple.

You rock!! Can't wait to be in your arms again.

xxxx

Almost 100kms

On January 9 of 2013 I downloaded a new running app, and without adding my January runs prior, I have almost hit a collective 100kms!

That's a bit cool.

It's amazing how the world feels closer to me these days as I connect with the ground and understand that distances are less than I first thought in my mind. Everything is within reach… or a run!

Today was a 7km jaunt in some light rain – beautiful. Afterwards, I felt ethereal, all blissed out and grateful.

I'm sure it's already been quoted somewhere in the world, but I thought of a saying today:

It's not a hill... it's a state of mind.

I strangely love running up hills and never focus on the top, just the little bit ahead of my feet with a few sideways glances around to catch any good views I might be missing. It's of course true for all the hills and hurdles in life. I *never* thought running would become such an emotional healer for me. It was never the intention.

Thanks to the Universe for the insight and wisdom, and for simply helping me move my feet with joy. Blessings. xxxx

First wintery kinda day

The view of our 'valley' today is just fog and rain.

Today's achievements are simply:

- keeping the fire stoked with wood
- hiding from the children in bed this morning with a magazine
- making plenty of cups of tea and coffee
- changing one children's DVD for another
- resting to stop myself coming down with a cold
- processing all the work I have done and have yet to do on a uni assignment
- stopping myself from bleeding all over the place due to a heavy, hurty period (sorry for TMI folk!)
- showing great enthusiasm for the girls' drawings and Lego buildings they're making by the fire
- not getting anyone dressed unless they feel like getting out of their pjs
- patting a smoochy puss-cat
- chatting on Skype and lazily searching online
- lying, sitting, or slouching wherever I feel like it
- *not* going outside

Thank goodness for days like this to make the world slow down a little. Life doesn't get any better, huh? Unless, of course, we had Kent here, too. xx

By the fire with the girls

Study success?

I know I haven't blogged much about uni yet as I have literally been in a panic about how to fit it into my life. So, rather than blogging about it, I've just been doing it.

Uni is so far amazing. I can actually say I love the two big, fat textbooks I've purchased. I wish I could curl up for days by the fire and read them (and more). Maybe that's a blessing because it's a treat to read rather than a duty. I literally don't have time to read normally, so building time into my life to read about self-discovery and people-skills is really enticing. No doubt in a few weeks, once I am forced to get through some quizzes, I may feel differently. But right now, I'm pumped!

The time at uni has been great, too.

The other students in my two subjects are a nice mix of folk. I have found myself feeling very enthusiastic about a few of them and think we'll establish a tight-knit student group that may become work colleagues/peers too. I've been careful not to disclose too much about myself – 'share don't scare', as they say, but I know I will open up as time passes.

I have changed over the last decade because originally, I would 'give away' my secrets far too quickly and feel awkward about it later on. Nowadays, I hold my cards a little closer, which isn't a bad thing. I am going into it with an open heart, but I'm also being a little more protective of myself until I need to share. Lessons have been learnt.

Anyway, enough time on this blasted screen.

We're heading out for dinner with friends and we're taking the tinlids – so wish us luck!

Blessings. x

My first Uni textbook

Positive reinforcement

Last night at uni we were given our first assignments back. They were only worth 10% and were just marked a non-graded pass or fail.

I was pretty confident I'd do ok until the lecturer started off by saying, "not everyone has passed", then my heart started thumping in my chest.

When I saw the 'NGP' on the front of mine, relief flooded through me. Then when I read through the comments, I had to stop myself from tearing up, I was so delighted.

It is meant to be. I can do this and do it well.

Fingers crossed I can continue with such amazing results, especially for the second assignment, which is worth 60% – I handed it in last night. Eek!

Sorry for my unashamed brag but here's a few of the comments from my lecturer.

'Congratulations, Ailsa, this paper was a joy to mark (you can teach the course next year). We would have awarded you a High Distinction in a graded marking system! Thank you.'

I know it's a bit over the top, but I'll take it! lol

Love to my ever-faithful readers and cheer squad. Hope you're getting HDs for everything in your lives right now, too! xxx

Post bushfire fall-out

I'm typing this with shaky fingers.

I'm feeling the fall-out after the bushfires close to our home over the weekend.

I packed in the quiet of the night alone with the kids asleep on Thursday as I peeked over the ridge at the massive orange glow of fire in the dark sky. I set my alarm hourly to check the CFS website, and it was getting worse, stating that homes could be lost before dawn.

Kent flew in from work into the flurry of action Friday morning.

We then evacuated and headed down with the kids, cat, photos, computers, etc., to my folks house a couple of towns away (a safer zone).

We went about our business, kept it all together. I played netball and we had a couple of great social nights with local friends in similar circumstances.

Mother's Day was glorious as we got to come home and also have a superb lunch at a local winery (Bird In Hand).

Last night, though, the minute I lay in my own bed I began to think and rethink all of what did happen or what could have happened. I just wanted the girls in bed next to me, close, so that everyone was within my arms' reach. I feel teary, I feel grateful, I feel raw. I am trembling, I feel anxious, I feel shattered.

Just needed to blog about it.

I know it's normal, I know it's ok, I know I'll come good soon.

But I also know the enormity of what we faced as a family and community on the weekend and we are all so lucky to have our lives, let alone our homes.

The fire was like a gigantic volcano spewing lava, apparently. The view across the affected valley was 180 degrees of flame. The smoke was overwhelming.

The stories I'm hearing about our local friends and neighbours doing brave acts to save properties makes me cry with love and thanks.

I think I need to let my tears wash away my worry, like the rain has washed away our danger from the fire.

This will no doubt help me in the future to counsel people who have faced similar situations.

In the meantime, I'll be kind to myself, cuddle my loved ones and send out gratitude to the Universe for the lessons I've learnt and, simply, for our lives.

Blessings and Love. xxx

Still shook up

Yesterday my body stopped trembling, but then came tears whilst unpacking the girls' clothes I'd chosen for them during the evacuation. Anger, too, has popped up; flashings of heat and frustration at the messiness of the disruption, and at the noise of children interrupting my jumbled thoughts.

I was also taken aback when my period started yesterday – six days early, no doubt brought on by stress as usually I am regular like clockwork.

So now I am weepy, bleeding, fiery, thankful, and very weary with a version of Lily's cold. Blurgh.

This morning I had to take Tess to childcare and then run a couple of errands including seeing my doctor for some scripts.

First, I was driving in a haze of thoughts about the weekend. The scent of smoke was caught in my car still and began being pumped around as the heaters warmed the cab. The scent immediately flashed me back to Thursday and Friday, packing back at the house whilst ash dropped from the sky. I then heard a chopper and again I was taken back to the choppers and water bombers over home and Uraidla. Finally, my gaze was drawn to rolling clouds and fog in the valley as I drove along, and I had to take a second look to clarify they weren't billowing clouds of smoke.

I can only imagine the extent of flashbacks people are having that fought those fires, and those so much closer that have just escaped with their homes and lives. The family that did lose their home is constantly in my mind, as too are my thoughts with their immediate neighbours that may be feeling a mix of relief and guilt that they still have their homes.

One of the workers at childcare said some of the kids that were evacuated and moved around a few times had been showing signs of distress. Thankfully my girls didn't question that we were sleeping over at Didi and Puppa's house, though Lily has seen photos on my computer and asked if they were of the fire (no doubt they know more than we think).

I was surprised by my GP's reaction when I explained how I felt. She agreed that yes, it must have been frightening, but then said to me: "imagine how you'd feel if you had lost your home or a loved one though" – simply dismissing my disclosure and that I was feeling affected by the ordeal. I just shut up then.

I've also been told by others that it is 'normal' and then been cut off.

I guess I feel I need a bit of help maybe, just to tell my story (hence my blogging again). Kent has been lovely with random hugs through my teary spells, but I probably seem a bit of a sook to him. I wonder if my experience as a child watching events during Ash Wednesday has stirred up my tears. I was in primary school and saw my classmates being pulled out of school one by one as their families were evacuating. My friend lost her home in the fires. Their family stayed with us for a few days. I remember everyone sitting in fogs of shock together in our lounge room.

We visited their burnt-out house and I remember there was a red plastic stool melted and warped in the middle of blackened ruins. I never really knew much about the people killed in those fires, as I was only a child, but many lived on that same street and some died there or in cars trying to flee down the hill.

Luckily the winds were in our favour and the conditions were mild.

The weekend's fire-fighting was run so professionally and on a huge scale. I have never seen so many emergency people and vehicles in one spot, including the chopper on our oval.

Many of our CFS mates fought the fire. My heart bursts with pride and thanks for them all. xx

The final straw for me coming home were the messages on our answering machine with the emergency warning siren and then details about evacuating.

The fire was close, the flames didn't get us but the fear of it has.

I can only imagine how haunted people are who have PTSD (post-traumatic stress disorder).

Blessings to all who are suffering.

xxx

One year since cosmetic surgery

It's a year today since I had my operation.

I made a brilliant decision when I booked my breast lift/tummy tuck. It was tough and I copped a fair dose of pain and discomfort during my healing process but it was all worth it. I'm still proud as punch of my awesome sitty-up boobs and if given another chance I'd do it all again.

I wonder what my surgeries will mean to my girls as they grow up. Will they look at my scarred body with a bit of horror like I did at my Nanna's scars.

I'll be honest with them about everything.

I will always encourage them to love their bodies including any imagined 'imperfections' or 'flaws', but if they do choose surgery in their futures, I'd support their decision.

Fucking Deets: looking at the wrong numbers!

I've just been having a look at my 'lovely' (not) diary of weekly weigh-in numbers and realised that maybe I've been looking at the wrong numbers!

Yes, the scales are saying I'm up slightly in weight, but I have very slowly slid down in fat percentage and slightly increased my muscle mass (so my new scales say). I have also noted that I cannot get close to my max heart rate on Keith when I'm doing interval training and that's apparently an indication of an increase in fitness.

I can also run further than ever and I'm the fittest I've been on the netball court since I was an early teenager. No wonder my pants feel good on me.

So once again the numbers have foiled me. I am not simply a number in kilos. I am all of the above.

In saying that, I do know I have increased my mindless eating since I've started studying – I've been on autopilot a lot. It was clear to me, though, on holiday in Brisbane that we maintain generally a really healthy diet at home. I felt like I had scurvy after five days of eating out, lol!

Perfect: who the FUCK are you and what do you ultimately want?

I glanced at my reflection in the kitchen window tonight. Compared to who I was a few years' ago, I'm all cheekbones, defined shoulders, no tum, and sitty-up boobs.

Who is this size-14 person? Who is this running, broccoli-loving, manic chick who still wants to be slimmer? What the fuck?

What about the sad girl who simply wanted to feel ok in a size 14-16. When was she left behind? This new chick smashed out a 6km-run yesterday and could have done it three times over if given the *time*.

I feel like sometimes I've been taken over by an alien. I am all black or white... have I eaten well, and worked out? Or, am I guzzling down the red wine and choc in a stupor?

Where is the grey? Where is the happy medium? I am medium right now, I guess – not plus-size, not small, just... medium. When will my head catch up and my heart just *let it be*.

You are good enough just as you are, Ailsa.

Stop fighting yourself. When will it be enough? When you can rock an evening frock and have the world at your feet? In reality, you don't have the baby sitters lined up to go out, or even the attention of a phantom crowd that you envisage will praise you as finally being 'just right'.

Nobody is interested anyway. They are just happy you are happy.

So just try and be that – happy. xx

Delayed gratification – is that what I've been working on?

I've been researching a topic for my next essay CBT & Obesity, looking at mindful/intuitive eating as being key to changing old, conditioned behaviours to new, intentional behaviours, and in doing so I've hit on the term 'delayed gratification'.

I guess it's what is behind so called 'will power', and I guess if you are a stubborn shit like I can be, you can use it to your benefit or detriment (bad = dieting).

I'm not sure what it means for me, but it seems like a bit of a light-bulb moment. I feel like I've been tweaking parts of myself that have moved me to live a healthier lifestyle. Impulse control is another factor. I still have a long way to go when it comes to my impulse control and angry outbursts, especially toward the kids when they are hammering at me, but I've done well in other areas.

My vices over the years have diminished. In fact, the ones I have left are decidedly tame most of the time... bar a hangover here and there!

Some lines I use all the time in my head that I think relate to delayed gratification are:

To food: *I can have it if I really want it, but do I really feel like it?* – from Dr Rick Kausman or *I can eat this another time and it will always be available, so let's wait until another day.*

To money: *Do I really need to buy this item? Can I make do with what I already have? What would I rather do with my money given the choice? (Go on a holiday!)*

To exercise: *A 30+ minute delay in my day is nothing, and I will never regret running/exercising. I'm going to allow myself to relax after this awesome workout and feel amazing.*

To household tasks and even studying: *A little time each day when you feel like sitting down and procrastinating will buy you a completed task and a clearer mind. Just do it – stop overthinking it!*

Even in conflict with others: *It's better to be kind than right. Don't just argue the point to make yourself feel you have won. Gracefully allowing the conflict to ebb naturally will make you feel better in the long run.*

Gratification, of course, always comes from being grateful in the present.

I feel grateful for all the knowledge I already have and all the knowledge I have deep in my soul still to be unlocked.

Blessings. xx

Bali

Bali was divine. The minute we arrived it smelt so familiar (clove cigarettes and incense), and the warmth of the air and the people made my heart instantly happy.

It was so wonderful to feel well and healthy on this holiday. I felt fit, lean, and confident in my body that has endured so much and has given me so much back including, of course, my most precious gifts – the girls.

When I was last in Bali I was around 15-16 years old, and also felt pretty spunky, but not nearly as confident and self-assured as I do now, of course. It's lovely to give thanks for the years of life-experience I have.

We had one of the best days at the Waterbomb park. The highlight (apart from donning a bikini top) was going on the waterslides – a huge deal for me after being scared for decades that I'd kill a small child if I landed on one at the end of a slide. PMSL!

My work here is done

Lily drew a picture at kindy today that made me so proud.

It was of Mummy running home in the rain.

I think I have normalised exercise in her eyes – this is just what her mummy does.

She asked to come running with me the other day. I'll maybe start with a walk and little bits of running, say up to the next tree, for instance, to build her confidence and the excitement of moving her body.

My heart is happy. Imagine if my girls both came on runs with me when they're older. No doubt they'll be more inclined to lay on the lounge, sulk, and swear like I did as a teenager. Ha.

A drawing of me running by Lily

A trophy?

Something very, very odd happened this weekend.

I received a Hills Netball Association trophy for runner-up Best & Fairest player in B1s.

What the...?!

Blow me down! I was shocked, elated, and humbled.

I have played netball off and on for 30+ years in the Hills Association for a couple of clubs. I haven't received an individual club trophy since I was about 12, I'd say. I've never been a stand-out player. Maybe I've had some great moments and I love being a positive force on the court amongst my team, but I haven't had this honour before.

The things you can do in your 40th year, huh?! The things you can do when you are mother of two and have never liked to run.

So enough about me. Thankfully, Miss Lil was there to see me get my trophy (Kent is away working and Tess was dropped off to my folks).

The Summertown Netball Tigers were all whooping and applauding like we'd won the Grand Final. Their love and support means the world to me. An extended group of sisters, really.

Never say never! Wow, the things you can achieve... even if you weren't trying to achieve them, ha!

Netball trophy

The past and the present

Sunday I'm running the 12km Adelaide City to Bay Funrun.

The last time I walked it and nearly died.

Back then I felt so self-conscious I wished the ground would swallow me. I used to wear oversized shirts over black pants and black tops – that was my uniform. I can't stand large shirts now. I would rather show a roll or two than wear a tent.

My ex ran the city to bay that same year in about two seconds. I cried when I finally finished, by myself, with chafing between my thighs and blisters all over my feet. The shame of how uncomfortably big and unfit I was, was probably the part that hurt most.

Last week I ran a lazy 7km while Kent rode his bike along with me. Fuck, I love feeling well and fit!

I'll be running for that girl in the past who wanted to howl all the way along the 12km-route about how unfair life was. It was a horrible part of my life, but my internal wishes and dreams were still to be manifested.

That past girl deserved all the love, light, support, and power this present girl has now – and then some!

Blessings & thanks, always. xxx

Achievement...

I ran the city to bay. I didn't walk a step. It was damn tough in parts, and a tad boring running in the city, but... I DID IT! I did it for myself. xx

Life is good.

Life is *very* good.

xxxx

Adelaide Hills spring walk

More good stuff

I'm in a muddle of assignments and life has been hectic with juggling uni and the kids whilst solo-parenting, but it's still been happy.

I'm feeling a little stiff after a run today and a bush walk through Morialta with a friend.

I'm so grateful, though, for all the little aches in my body because it means I've moved it, and what beautiful views to take in on the journey!

"Wear clothes that make you feel great, do things that make you feel brave, and make choices that bring you joy."

Wonderful words. I liked the brave bit the best.

Hope this finds you being brave, feeling joyous, and rocking an outfit that makes you feel FAB!

Loves. xxxx

2014

OUT OF STEAM...

Insight number one – grief can creep up on you

My beautiful Gramps, John Robson, passed away on Wednesday the 8th of January.

I am very sad even though I thought I was prepared for his death.

He was, after all, in his 102nd year. What a remarkable (and as he would say), probably ridiculous age to live to.

He was a gentleman, with a sharp mind until the very end, keeping interested in life events and especially interested in his family.

He taught me a great deal about how to be courteous. His manners were impeccable.

Farewell my beautiful Gramps. I will sacredly remember singing *You are my sunshine* together with you, Tess and Lily in the last month of your life. You lit up watching those great-grandbabes of yours.

We are blessed to have had you in our lives.

I love you so very much. You were a wonderful, loving grandfather and friend.

xxxxx

My body is giving away it's grief.

I have been calm and unaltered mostly but now I feel I am showing my pain like a rag being wrung...

Dry it seems, until a twist of memory wrings out a splutter of tears and gasps.

Then as quick as it comes the thought subsides and I am seemingly dry until the next loaded memory rises.

Once done, the stinging salty marks on my face are all that is left.

I'm empty.

I wrote this in bed as I lay there struggling with waves of grief before I fell asleep one night.

Bless all those that are facing any kind of grief – I send you all my love. xxx

Insight number two – fat is frightening

I have run once in two months and worked out on Keith once this year.

I have been living it up over the festive season and drinking and eating for happiness and sadness over this time.

I have gained quite a lot of weight, so the scales say – pffft!

I have also found some of my clothes slightly squeezy in places I don't wish to be squeezed. Even my flatish tum is rounding (though still neatly it seems), and I would say my breasts are blooming.

This is all well and good to say in jest but the fear of this enveloping fat is making me feel quite claustrophobic. How scary is it to feel smothered by yourself? Fucking scary really!

I have been good at resisting the flood of diet/workout new year bullshit propaganda and even discussions with random people who have found their own new 'best diet/health plan'. Pat on the back to me.

I do, however, understand that action needs to occur in my life.

So I am reflecting on what's not working for me and re-authoring my story (I'm studying narrative therapy at the mo', and it rocks!).

I have come back to four key principles:
- Check in on your hunger
- Eat until you are satisfied, not completely full
- Eat to feel well
- Move your body – in fact sweat happily daily

All of them are underpinned by love and being kind to myself.

All of them are achievable.

Today I have started my new year with a workout on Keith to remind myself that just 25 mins in interval mode – 30-second sprint, 90-second recovery makes me sweat and happy.

I can afford myself 25 mins daily. xx

This too shall pass, and I shall be feeling back to my fit and fab self very soon, I'm sure.

Much love to all those with bodies they aren't 100% happy with for whatever reason – remember that you are PERFECT and exactly as you should be today. The Universe is providing you with all you need – love, lessons, gifts, hope, and passion. xxx

Insight number three – life moves fast!

Life certainly is what happens when you're busy making other plans, thanks Lennon.

'Life' has remarkably been happening to us over these past few weeks/months and I haven't had a chance to document much of it, or indeed give thanks for all the big and small sparkling moments that have occurred – they have been numerous. I am blessed.

I want to post an epiphany I just had (whilst blow drying my hair and squealing happily to myself).

I am doing my Masters, and I am getting distinctions and high distinctions for my assignments, even through some particularly shitty times.

WHAT THE??!!

Family time with Kent, my Aunty Jill and Uncle Noel

I think it has just dawned on me that I may have some good stuff in this messed up noggin' of mine and, more to the point, once the slog in Academia-land passes, I shall have a sweet little parchment and hopefully a heart and soul full of hope for future clients.

Blessed, that is what I am. Blessed.

So tonight, a big glass of celebratory wine for today's Attachment assignment result will be had. I was happy with a P after needing an extension, but received a D! Yay *squeal!*

....

2014 was the end of my blog posts. Studying my Masters degree had consumed me, and life as a FIFO family was taking its toll. It was too raw to write about. Instead, we were swept along in an intense wave until 2017 when Kent retired from any further work in the mining industry and came home to us ♥

The four of us in 2014

PRESENT DAY REFLECTIONS

I knew I was on a journey of self-discovery. I wanted to be at a more comfortable weight, so I focussed on weight-loss with the understanding there were emotional landmines scattered throughout the process. I had tried diet after diet, and I had begun to understand the diets had actually failed *me* (not the other way around). Still, the intoxicating lure of checking my worth against the scales was too seductive.

Hindsight is a wonderful thing. I can see I was questioning my identity as a mother of young children. I felt uncomfortable that I wasn't in the paid workforce and contributing financially to our family. I lived an often very lonely, solo life, as my husband worked in the mining industry – flying-in and flying-out. I felt many aspects in my life were out of my control but felt the one thing I could control to a certain degree was my weight. Of course, that was a fallacy.

My body-image struggles are clearly on display throughout my blog posts. The influence of intergenerational and cultural notions of my body being deemed 'good enough' is something I will no doubt explore for the rest of my life. I don't blame anyone for my anguish over my body image – those who influenced me over the years were simply doing their best with the influences they had in their own lives. My stories are merely my version of truth, and will no doubt be perceived differently by others. One thing I have learnt is that it is ok to have different perspectives.

I own how I feel about myself and I have stopped apologising for the space I take up. I am a sassy, curvaceous, intelligent, kind, and generous woman. I will never ask my children to apologise for their bodies. They are worthy and loved just the way they are – always.

Using reflection, contemplation, and self-compassion whilst journaling helped to change the way I viewed myself. Incorporating joyful movement into my days is the biggest, most self-loving change I have made. Counting my blessings daily brings calm into my world.

The knowledge I now hold due to my fascination with research, and the conversations being had in the worldwide HAES community is a gift. The gift is universal acceptance of myself, and all people living in all sorts of bodies.

It aligns with one of the main values in my life: kindness. I always aim to be kind to others and kind to myself. That doesn't mean I always get it right, but when I get it wrong, I acknowledge it and give thanks for the lessons I learn.

There are judgey parts of me that have popped up as I've collated this book; my older self who is more educated and very pissed off with her younger, naive self, and also my older and *wiser* self that is willing to give younger Ailsa a break – she was just learning, in her own space, with the tools she had at hand, whilst trying to be the best person, partner and mother she could be.

There's plenty of time for further self-exploration. In the meantime, though, I'll keep adding more self-compassion to my life. I am worthy just as I am, flaws and all. And so are *you*.

I hope after reading my book there have been moments where you felt a connection. Has anything shifted for you? Are you looking at yourself slightly differently in the mirror? Or, are you beginning to say kinder things to yourself? I can only wish that you do not feel alone with your thoughts. This book has already generated interest from readers to develop a community of sorts – a *Perfectly Imperfect community*. How that plays out will be seen in the future.

In the meantime, you can keep in touch with me via my website **ailsarobson.com**

Take good care of you. xx

Onwards and Upwards.

Much love and blessings, Ailsa. x

I was asked by one of my readers to explain what happened during my transition to weight neutrality; from wanting my body to be thinner to being comfortable with my body as it is now.

It was a brilliant, blindingly obvious question that needed to be answered.

So what did happen?

- I grew up and grew in my knowledge.
- I realised I wasn't the centre of the universe – to me, my kids are.
- I began to believe that my weight didn't equal my worth – who I am as a person is most important.
- I stopped taking myself and my body so seriously.
- I stopped believing the media, and that diet-culture is normal.
- I began to listen to, and seek out stories from other large, fit, happy, intelligent, strong, empowered women who don't engage with diet-culture.
- I touched base with other bloggers who had weight-loss surgery and who were still struggling psychologically with their body image regardless of their weight-loss.
- I started to rebel against what I thought my larger body couldn't do, and I began to move my body for joy.
- I began to realise that my healthy behaviours, not weight, make me a healthier person.
- I began believing in myself regardless of mistakes and setbacks.
- I stopped listening to my family's stories about what constitutes a 'good body'.
- I got mad, then empowered about rightfully taking up space in the world.
- I educated myself further in *Health At Every Size®* principles.
- I brought more self-compassion into my life and gifted myself more love, time and movement.
- I let myself be vulnerable whilst reflecting on my life.
- I was brave even when I was scared.
- I inspired others to find their own power and I realised that I was born to be an advocate.

So this is me, in my present life:
- I refuse to diet or engage in diet-culture talk.
- I trust my body's internal cues and respond to them with intuitive attention – e.g. I eat when I am hungry, I eat what I desire, and foods and amounts that leave me feeling *well*.
- I notice what my body needs: sleep, water, rest, play, sunshine – and tend to it.
- I notice my feelings and how they relate to my body's needs – e.g. sometimes I am sad and want to just eat cheese toasties and that's ok.
- Often I stuff up, don't check-in properly with myself, and eat foods or amounts that don't make me feel great and that's ok too – I am human.
- I shake my body, move my curvy, strong self and rejoice in the movement that I participate in.
- I don't apologise for any foods that I may consume, or for days I may miss moving my body.
- I try to consider myself more kindly, and not apologise for the way I look. I may feel shitty at times, but I know the feeling will pass. I know I am so much more than my physical body.
- I incorporate humour into almost everything I do. Life is short – laugh out loud!
- I believe in people, I really do, regardless of the dumb stuff we all do.
- I will accept you for you – full stop.
- I won't take crap though; I am a Tiger (like my Chinese zodiac – not like figuratively), so watch yourself – ha, growl.
- I will listen to your stories, but I will not take on your 'stuff' – that's yours to own.
- I give the bird to unhelpful thoughts; they are just thoughts, not truths.
- I love people madly – family, friends, clients, community, peers.

Photo by Allison Hernach

JAN 2018

I AM WORTHY OF THIS SPACE

'I am worthy of this space' is what I kept repeating in my mind today as I moved around in a bikini on the beach. I am worthy of taking up my spot on the sand regardless of the well-known terrified voice in my head, the voice that spits through gritted teeth 'people are going to SEE you, see your enormous dimpled thighs and skin that wobbles'.

My new voice calmly but sternly said, 'Let. Them. See.'

I will no longer be held ransom by my inner mean girl. My sassy gal tossed off her towel, took a deep breath and walked strongly into the water toward my gorgeous young daughters who haven't yet created their own internal, damning whispers. They just know their bodies through glorified skinned knees and bike-stack bruises... not through self-questioning about whether they are 'good enough' to wear a bikini.

I will keep showing up and wearing clothes that make me feel beautiful and comfortable even with my extra curves on show. I am worthy of the space in which I stand. It's taken me many moons of personal reflections to get me to this place, and it's life-long work. I do it for my beautiful children, and for anyone who second-guesses living a vibrant life full of fabulous experiences because of their encroaching inner critic. You are worthy. You are good enough.

Along with beautifully-exfoliated sand-kissed feet, salty eyelashes and a massive grin on my face, I also came away from the beach with a splendid shell. It is cracked and tumbled but I love it as it's 'perfectly imperfect'.

So today was anything but imperfect – it was a stunning diamond day with my gorgeous family. Here's to showing up and knowing you are worthy! Ailsa. x

Ailsa Robson – Counsellor and Psychotherapist.
Skype / One on One / Walk and Talk Therapy
Adelaide Hills, South Australia. **www.ailsarobson.com**

PLACE AND PRIVILEGE

Throughout my writing I speak of my local area, the Adelaide Hills.

I wish to acknowledge the Peramangk Aboriginal people whose traditional lands I have grown up on, become a mother on and now raise my children on. I often think of the Aboriginal women who, too, have mothered and lived on my hill, and then I think of the women settlers and generations of local women who have birthed and raised their families in these hills, in my family home in Uraidla, and on the beautiful piece of land I live on now. I pay homage to those women and thank them for their spirit and energy that still lives around me, reminding me to be thankful for place, belonging and for love.

I do not take lightly the life that I lead and that is why throughout the journey of collating this book I felt my privilege was never acknowledged within the words. I understand that all of my reflections have come from the privileged perspective of a woman who is white, educated, financially secure, straight, partnered with children and with an able body that is deemed larger than 'normal' but not stigmatised as much as bodies larger than mine. I acknowledge the marginalisation of people living different realities to mine. I hope that readers can see that my self-reflection comes with awareness of my own perception. This is my story, written initially for myself, but is now being offered to the world. I am still learning about my own privilege, as I am learning about all of what I mused about in my writing. I know it is life-long work and I am willing to be humbled by it.

Photo by Meaghan Coles

ABOUT THE AUTHOR

Ailsa Robson is a water baby, incessant muser and writer, and someone who always looks for the silver lining. She lives in the Adelaide Hills, South Australia, with her loves – husband Kent, daughters Lily and Tess, and alley cat, Gus. She has a private Psychotherapy and Counselling practice and is a passionate *Health At Every Size®* advocate.

Ailsa's understanding and empathy for those who need support, has intensified through her experience in the Community Care sector over the last twenty years. Her love for community, in all its forms, and her belief in the power of belonging and connecting, spurs her to volunteer her time on committees and projects. Her natural energy, plus years of public speaking, have made Ailsa a genuine and charismatic speaker. Her university degrees are an eclectic mix; and although she is not an anthropologist or librarian (though qualified), she is certainly a professional in the mental health field after completing her Masters Degree in Counselling and Psychotherapy. This degree tested her circus skills, as she completed placement whilst renovating her home and living in a shed with her two young daughters and an often-absent husband due to his FIFO* work commitments.

Ailsa popped out the other side to create a unique business/lifestyle where she shimmies to the beat of her own tambourine. Her love of collaboration and pushing boundaries has led her to offer Walk and Talk Psychotherapy, and to base her practice in the gym where she works out with a community of passionate people.

Ailsa specialises in helping folk who feel stuck in stories of not being good enough, and provides compassionate, heartfelt, person-centred counselling that is uniquely tailored to her clients. She can generally be found shaking her butt in less than sharp active-wear, grinning like a Cheshire cat, and building up those around her. When she's not doing that, you'll find her blissing out by the ocean... musing again.

www.ailsarobson.com

ACKNOWLEDGMENTS

Thank you to my parents for being my unwavering supporters and toughest critics – the salt balances the sweet. I love you with utter abandon.

And Di, it is always your passionate lead I follow – even without realising. I don't know who I'd be without you.

Kent (Baby), thank you for being there as I wept with vulnerability whilst compiling this book, and for always believing in me. I love you.

To my family, scattered throughout states. Thank you for indulging me as I yet again stomped off into unknown territory, and for lovingly taking my calls and emails when I felt a bit lost.

To each of my dear generous friends who have helped mould this book through feedback and their own personal reflections. Thank you for investing in a gazillion discussions about the book with me, and for the constant encouragement.

Thanks especially to Leonie Marks, Tania Erzinger, Clarissa Terry, Cate Howell, Susan Williams, Cate Walsh, Jane Aufderheide, Renee Stratton, Julie Piantadosi, Sarah Roberts, Amanda Spedding and Sophie White for your invaluable feedback.

I have immense respect for my generous, authentic and skilled book publishing consultant, Julie Postance, who guided me perfectly with *Perfectly Imperfect*. Thank you so much, Julie.

I give thanks for the women in my life who have shaped me: grandmothers, mothers, aunts, daughters, sisters, nieces, soul-sisters; and for the good men behind them. I am blessed.

My friends are my family. My community is my core.

REFERENCES

Books

If Not Dieting, Then What by Rick Kausman

Health At Every Size by Linda Bacon

Eat What You Love, Love What You Eat by Michelle May

Eating In The Light Of The Moon by Anita A Johnston

Eat Pray Love by Elizabeth Gilbert

Buddism for Mothers by Sarah Naphtali

Birthing From Within by Pam England & Rob Horowitz

When Your Kids Push Your Buttons by Bonnie Harris

Mining Families Rock – Your complete guide to healthy relationships, happy kids and a household that works from the creators of Mining Family Matters.

Films/TV

The Boys Are Back

United States of Tara

Jaws

USEFUL LINKS

ASDAH: HAES® Principles
www.sizediversityandhealth.org/content.asp?id=76

HAES® Australia
www.haesaustralia.org.au

HAES ® Community
haescommunity.com

If Not Dieting Then What?®
www.ifnotdieting.com.au

Parenting in a Disordered Eating Ecosystem
https://more-love.org/

Susan Williams -Zest Nutrition
www.zestnutrition.com.au

Leonie Marks
www.thesoulwhisperer.com.au

Dianne McCann Mathews
www.beyondtheordinary.net.au

Dr Cate Howell
www.drcatehowell.com.au

Jane Aufderheide
www.playtimemarket.com.au

Julie Piantadosi
juliemotivate.com

Mining Family Matters
www.miningfm.com.au

GLOSSARY OF TERMS

For those folk, like my parents, who may not be used to reading blogs 😉

FIFO
Fly-In Fly-Out

HAES®
Health At Every Size®

LOL
Laugh out loud

TMI
Too much information

BTW
By the way

PMSL
Pee myself laughing

OMG
Oh my god

MORE FROM AILSA ROBSON

www.ailsarobson.com

Instagram: @ailsa_robson

Facebook: Ailsa Robson Consulting

Twitter: @Ailsa_Robson

www.ingramcontent.com/pod-product-compliance
Lightning Source LLC
Chambersburg PA
CBHW020231170426
43201CB00007B/383